CLASSIC OLD HOUSE PLANS

THREE CENTURIES OF AMERICAN DOMESTIC ARCHITECTURE

CLASSIC OLD HOUSE PLANS

THREE CENTURIES OF AMERICAN DOMESTIC ARCHITECTURE

BY LAWRENCE GROW

THE MAIN STREET PRESS • PITTSTOWN, NEW JERSEY

Copyright © 1978, 1984 by The Main Street Press

Published by
The Main Street Press, Inc.
William Case House
Pittstown, New Jersey 08867

Distributed in the United States by
Kampmann & Company, Inc.
9 East 40th Street
New York, New York 10016

Published simultaneously in Canada by
Methuen Publications
2330 Midland Avenue
Agincourt, Ontario M1S 1P7

Cover design by Frank Mahood

Printed in the United States of America

Text design by Denise Ingrassia

Library of Congress Cataloging in Publication Data

Grow, Lawrence, 1939-

   Classic old house plans; three centuries of American
domestic architecture.

   1. Architecture, Domestic—United States—Designs and
plans.   I. Title.
NA7205.G768   1984   728.3′7′0222   84-881
ISBN 0-915590-41-7 (pbk.)

Contents

Architectural history is the story of styles, materials, and methods. It is of necessity approached in a case-by-case fashion. Just as the student of law studies the great arguments of the past and the decisions reached by eminent jurists, the formal study of architecture requires a knowledge of what constitutes the best in building design and how this was achieved. Little attention is paid to the failures or even the commonplace. The vast majority of the old houses in which people live today, nevertheless, are of the commonplace sort. One hundred years ago they might even have been considered failures. They are vernacular renderings of classically defined styles. The history of great houses and their master designers has been written many times; the vernacular dwelling, often the work of a carpenter-builder, is rarely studied or explained. With the growth of an historical preservation movement which encompasses much more than the masterpieces or the historically-important George-Washington-Slept-Here kind of house, information on what was done on the everyday level is badly needed. Almost any building which has managed to survive the mad pursuit of material progress in North America is surely deserving of such study. *Classic Old House Plans* seeks to meet that need.

Various builders' handbooks and compilations of designs have been reprinted in recent years. These are of inestimable value in documenting the history of a popular style and may even provide specific details which aid those seeking to restore or otherwise preserve a period building. Circulation of these reprints, however, has been limited to a fairly small circle of enthusiasts. They are the first to agree that the time has arrived to disseminate this material in more popular form.

Classic Old House Plans covers thirteen domestic building styles popular at various times in North America from the mid-1600s to the mid-1900s. Elevations, floor plans, perspectives, and detail drawings of individual homes—many of which have been drawn from contemporary sources as well as from the files of the Historic American Buildings Survey (*see* Sources)—are given as illustrations of the development and use of specific architectural forms and elements. Where interior arrangements are known, these are specified. None of the examples can be considered typical in every respect. The "average" house does not exist. But there is enough which is stylistically common about the examples to offer them as sound guidelines.

"Colonial," like "Victorian," is a stylistic term which defies precise definition. The Colonial aesthetic as practiced by pre-Revolutionary carpenters, builders, and architects varied widely from colony to colony and even within the provincial boundaries of the time. At least five distinct "Colonial" styles have been recognized by historians—Spanish, New England, Southern, French, and Dutch. Domestic Colonial architecture in America was of a vernacular sort; to what extent the practitioners of the style followed a dictated sense of principles is nearly impossible to determine in most of their buildings. After the mid-eighteenth century, it is clear that there was some reliance on rule and pattern books, but the design and construction of all but the most expensive homes were at best informal undertakings.

Each generation of Americans since the Revolution has considered the Colonial style in terms of a particular time and place. To small-time farmers or craftsmen building new homes in sparsely populated areas during the first half of the nineteenth century, the Colonial form was the one they knew and held on to as traditional. It was also affordable. To the newly-rich merchants of East Coast cities in the 1820s and '30s, Colonial was an "old-fashioned" form best left to the past and replaced with the more decorative and classical forms of the Greek or Gothic Revivals. By the 1880s, however, Americans of the middle and upper classes were beginning to indulge a nostalgia for their Colonial past. A swing away from the Victorian Gothic and Queen Anne styles was clearly evident by the 1890s. Loose interpretations of seventeenth- and eighteenth-century forms—including the Spanish, New England, and Southern Colonial—constituted what is now known as the "Colonial Revival," and this trend has continued in vernacular architecture to the present.

Throughout the seventeenth and eighteenth centuries the Colonial style was in a state of constant development. Firmly rooted in medieval building practices, it reached its most sophisticated expression in the great use of brick, elaborate wood millwork, and expanded dimensions during the Georgian period of the mid- to late-eighteenth century. Although it is impossible to designate as the ultimate word in "Colonial" the building forms of seventeenth- and eighteenth-century Virginia, or New Jersey, or Connecticut (much less the ersatz reproductions of these in knotty-pine twentieth-century style), it is possible to decipher certain characteristics which remained relatively constant over a long period of time. We are, of course, dealing here with generalizations; anyone seeking to restore a Colonial dwelling must refer to specifics of a given time and area.

The first dwellings were unadorned and structurally simple. Those that remain today are praised for their directness, their honesty. Most settlers built only what they could afford with materials readily at hand and in a style with which they were already familiar. This meant in most cases a dwelling of one and a half or two stories which was probably only one room deep. The first "center-hall" Colonials contained two rooms on the principal floor, one of which served as a kitchen and the other as a parlor. In New England, one chimney of stone and plaster rose in the center of the house and usually contained two fireplaces, one for each of the two principal rooms. In the South and in areas settled by the Dutch and Germans in the Middle Atlantic states, the fireplaces were usually placed on the gable ends of the house. The second floor, if more than an attic, provided sleeping as well as storage space. It was common practice, however, for beds to be set up on the first floor. Both parlor and kitchen, sometimes termed the "hall," were true family rooms of the time. Many houses contained a cellar which was at least half the size of the house.

The majority of the homes were of wood, some of stone, and a few of brick, that material being a much more expensive medium in which to build. The familiar image of a clapboard structure is not a twentieth-century invention; the exterior walls of many early houses were covered in this manner. Clapboards, usually of oak until late in the Colonial period when pine came into use, were an improvement on the broader weatherboards which had been used earlier in England and on the Continent to protect plastered walls. Oak and pine were also employed in the interior in the form of wainscoting and completely paneled walls. Paint was rarely used; plaster walls were merely whitewashed. Glass came into currency slowly, and at first could be afforded only by the wealthy. Window openings, small by necessity, were closed up by the use of wooden shutters or in combination with cloth or oiled paper. Double sashes were a mid-eighteenth century improvement; casement windows were the early norm.

The first weather-beaten Colonials were, then, extremely primitive structures; they can be called picturesque today. They bear little resemblance—except in their box-like profiles—to the comfortably furnished and well-tended dwellings featured in *Yankee, Antiques,* or *Southern Living.* Colonial-style dwellings which have not been "improved" in some way, however, are difficult to find. While closet stairs or tightwinders and oppressively low ceilings may remain in many small dwellings, the majority of such homes were altered during the Colonial period and, of course, later. The most common addition to the basic two-room dwelling was the lean-to on the back or the addition of an ell. At the same time these changes were being made, entirely new houses, two rooms deep, were being built.

The four Colonial-style homes shown on the following pages date from the mid-1700s to the early 1800s. All are considerably more spacious and elaborate in design than buildings of the earlier years of settlement. The Vallé House (pp. 10-12) in the historic Ste. Genevieve community of Missouri was built by a prosperous man whose wealth came from early mining ventures. Yet the structure is typical in form of many modest French Colonial dwellings—low-slung, with a very steep gable roof and chimneys at each gable end. The first floor originally consisted of four rooms with an open porch behind them; this last space has since been completely enclosed for use as a kitchen and breakfast room. The second floor is hardly more than a room deep; dormers cut out of the roof line provide extra space. The design, while finely executed, is basically utilitarian.

The Justin Williams House (p. 13) on Cape Cod, Massachusetts, is representative of the expanded classical New England clapboard dwelling. The floor plan of the original square building has been considerably altered over the years. Built with a massive center chimney to serve the main parlor and kitchen, the house was enlarged by the addition of two ells later in the 1800s. The principal rooms, however, with the exception of the expanded old kitchen, remain quite small; the floor-to-ceiling height is only 8′2½″. The ceilings of the original section are plastered, the walls are wainscoted, and the floors are random-width pine.

Both the Chase-Lloyd House in Annapolis and Blandfield, in rural Virginia, typify the best in Georgian Colonial design. William Buckland, one of the most accomplished architects of the 18th century, was responsible for at least the interior design of the Annapolis town house and may have completed the exterior as well. He is also thought to have influenced the design of Blandfield. Both the Chase-Lloyd House (p. 14), seen without its later addition, and the main façade of Blandfield (p. 16) feature central Palladian pavilions which project slightly outward. Two massive chimneys are positioned on hip-on-hip roofs. In each case, the first-floor plan of the main block consists of a center hall and four principal rooms. The major design differences between the two dwellings—the number of floors and arrangement of secondary rooms—derive from their intended use. The Chase-Lloyd House is an urban town house that was occupied only intermittently by an Eastern Shore planter family; Blandfield,

the home of the Beverlys, was built as their principal plantation residence, with service buildings or dependencies connected to the main house by what are known architecturally as "hyphens" or wide passageways.

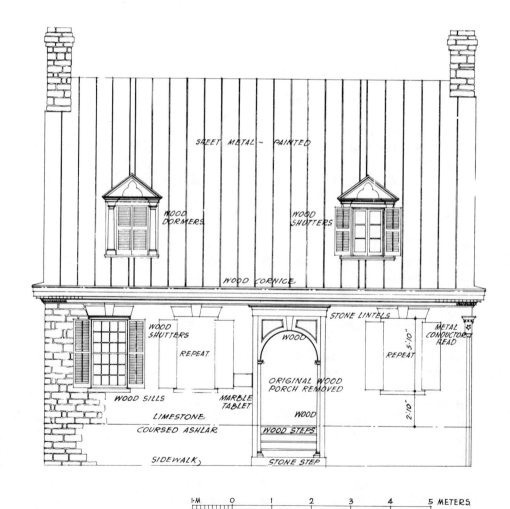

Felix and Odille Pratte Vallé House, Ste. Genevieve, Missouri, 1764, north elevation.

Sectional view (east).

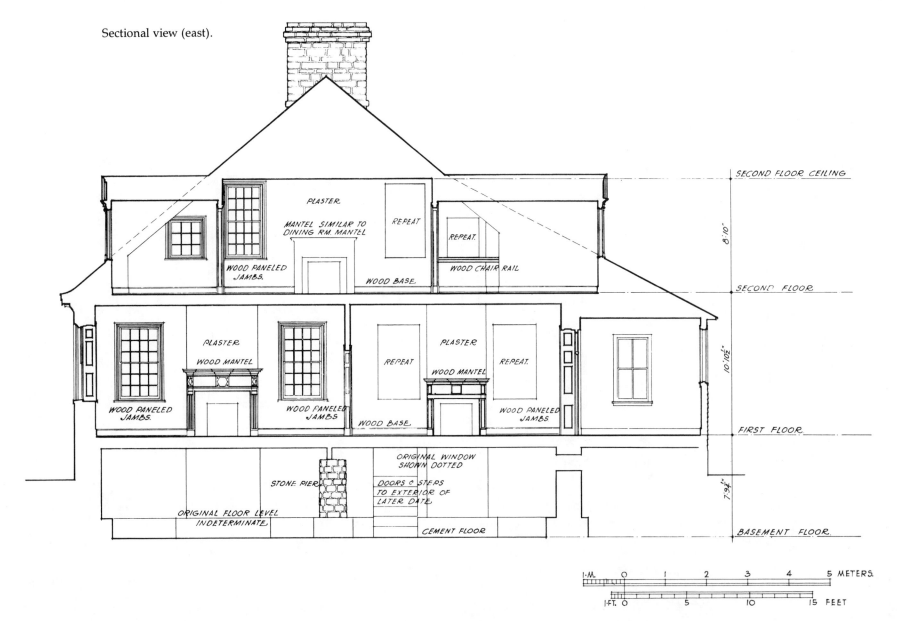

SECOND FLOOR CEILING

PLASTER.

MANTEL SIMILAR TO
DINING RM. MANTEL

REPEAT

REPEAT.

8'-10"

WOOD PANELED
JAMBS.

WOOD BASE

WOOD CHAIR RAIL

SECOND FLOOR.

PLASTER

WOOD MANTEL

REPEAT

PLASTER

WOOD MANTEL

REPEAT.

10'-10½"

WOOD PANELED
JAMBS.

WOOD PANELED
JAMBS.

WOOD BASE.

WOOD PANELED
JAMBS.

FIRST FLOOR.

ORIGINAL WINDOW
SHOWN DOTTED

STONE PIER.

DOORS & STEPS
TO EXTERIOR OF
LATER DATE.

7'-9¼"

ORIGINAL FLOOR LEVEL
INDETERMINATE.

CEMENT FLOOR

BASEMENT FLOOR.

1·M.   0   1   2   3   4   5 METERS.

1·FT. 0   5   10   15 FEET

First-floor plan.

Second-floor plan.

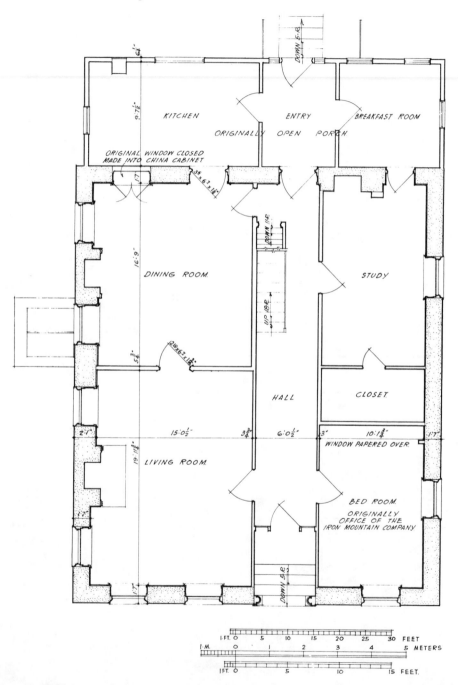

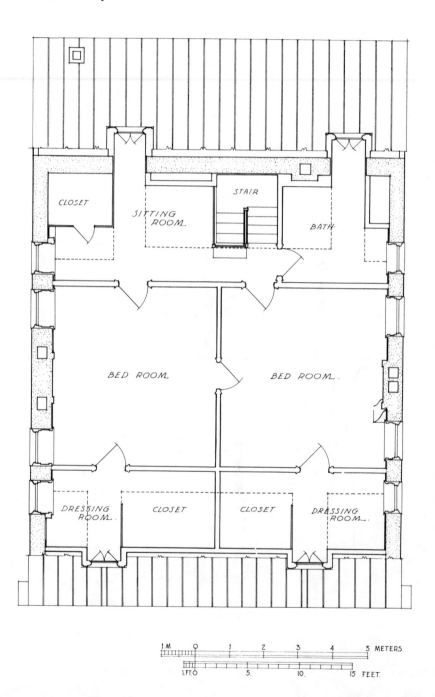

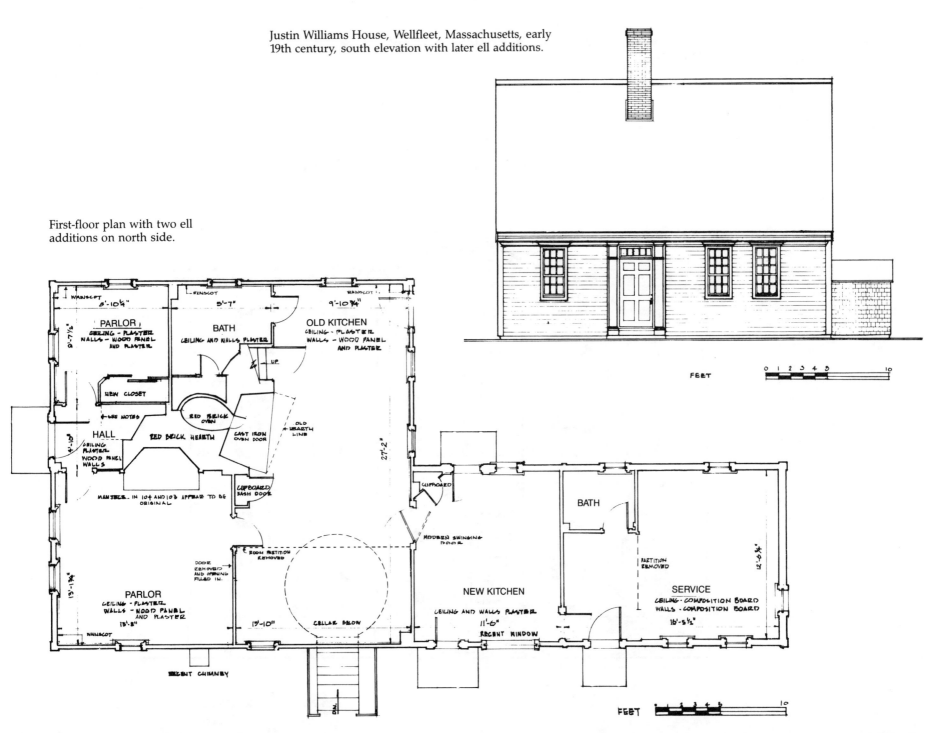

Justin Williams House, Wellfleet, Massachusetts, early 19th century, south elevation with later ell additions.

First-floor plan with two ell additions on north side.

PARLOR
CEILING - PLASTER
WALLS - WOOD PANEL
AND PLASTER

WAINSCOT 8'-10¼"

WAINSCOT 5'-7"

WAINSCOT 9'-10¾"

BATH
CEILING AND WALLS PLASTER

OLD KITCHEN
CEILING - PLASTER
WALLS - WOOD PANEL
AND PLASTER

NEW CLOSET

← SEE NOTES

UP

RED BRICK OVEN

HALL
CEILING
PLASTER
WOOD PANEL
WALLS

RED BRICK HEARTH

CAST IRON OVEN DOOR

OLD HEARTH LINE

CUPBOARD SASH DOOR

MANTELS IN 104 AND 103 APPEAR TO BE ORIGINAL

27'-2"

CUPBOARD

MODERN SWINGING DOOR

BATH

DOOR REMOVED AND OPENING FILLED IN

ROOM PARTITION REMOVED

PARTITION REMOVED

12'-0¾"

PARLOR
CEILING - PLASTER
WALLS - WOOD PANEL
AND PLASTER
13'-8"

13'-1¾"

WAINSCOT

17'-10"

CELLAR BELOW

NEW KITCHEN
CEILING AND WALLS PLASTER
11'-6"
RECENT WINDOW

SERVICE
CEILING - COMPOSITION BOARD
WALLS - COMPOSITION BOARD
16'-5½"

RECENT CHIMNEY

DN.

FEET 0 1 2 3 4 5 10

FEET 0 1 2 3 4 5 10

Chase-Lloyd House, Annapolis, Maryland, 1769-74, southeast
elevation.

0 2 4 6 8 10 12 14 16 FT.

Elevation and plan of main entrance.

First-floor plan.

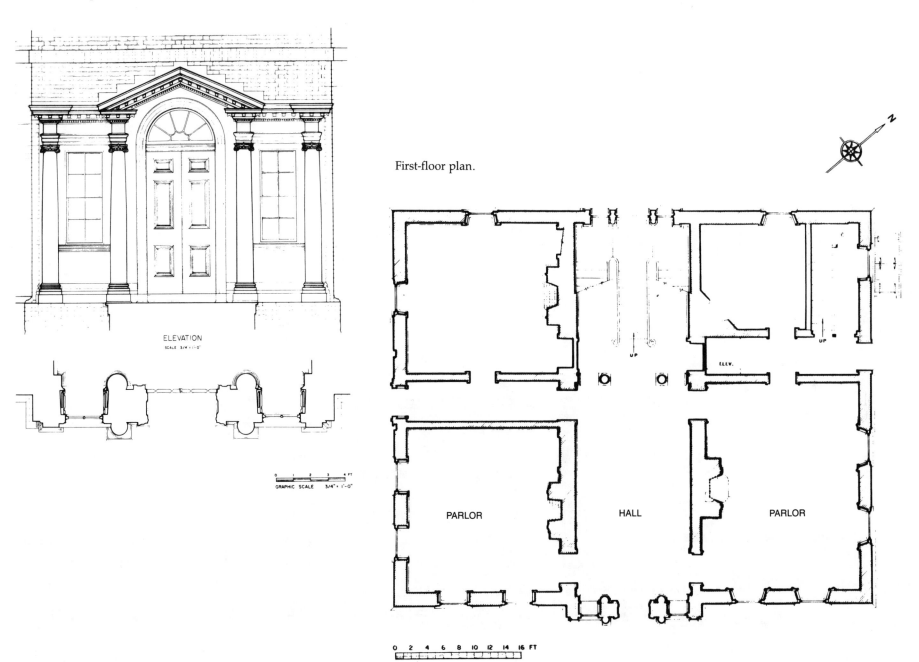

ELEVATION
SCALE 3/4" = 1'-0"

0 1 2 3 4 FT
GRAPHIC SCALE 3/4" = 1'-0"

PARLOR

HALL

PARLOR

ELEV.

UP

UP

0 2 4 6 8 10 12 14 16 FT

Blandfield, Tappahannock vicinity, Virginia, 1769-73, main block, west elevation.

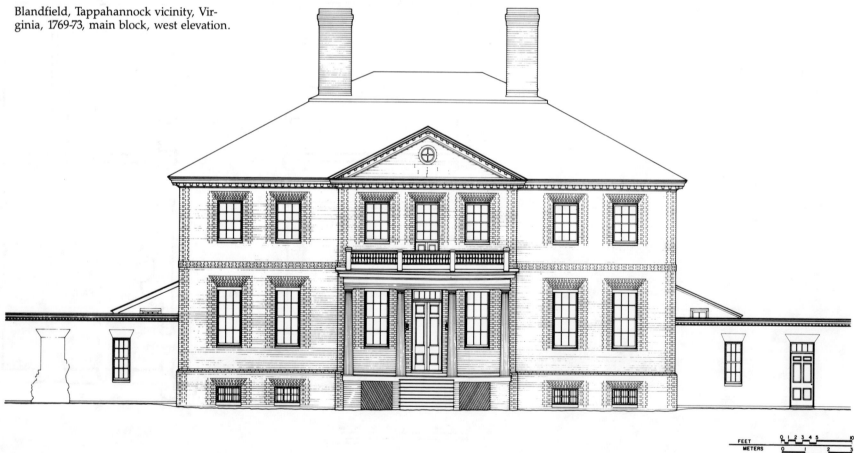

FEET
METERS

First-floor plan and complete west elevation.

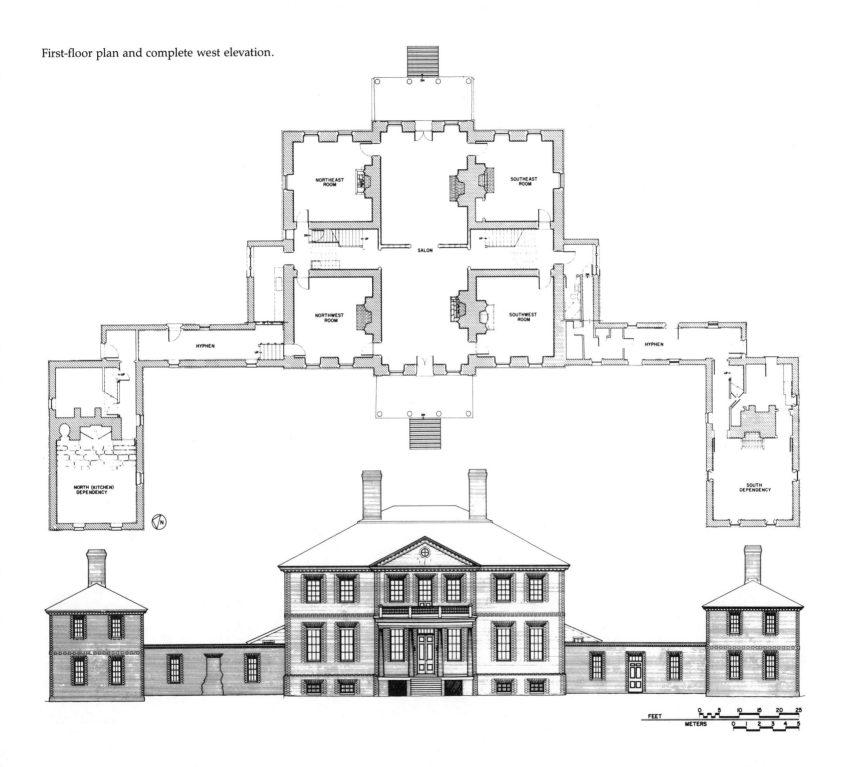

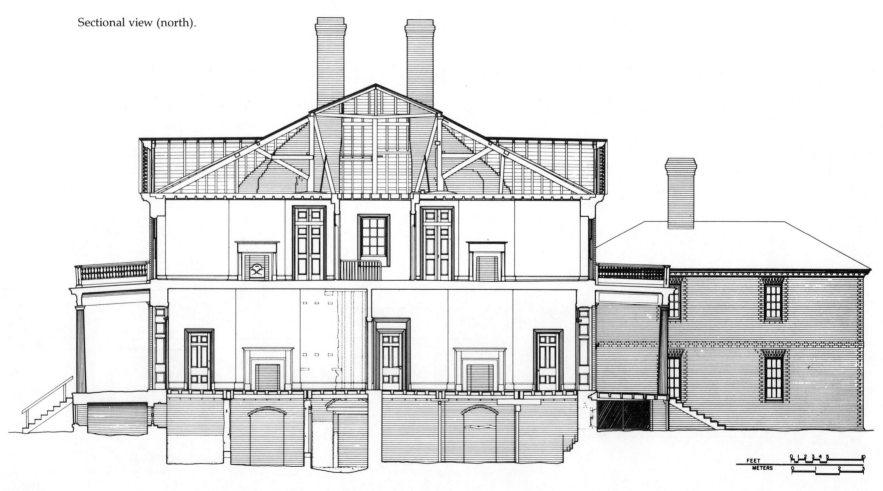

Sectional view (north).

Second-floor plan, main block.

Typical interior door,
first floor, main block.

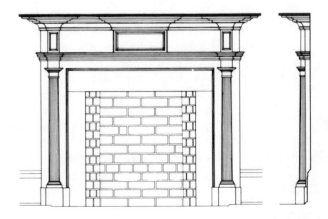

Mantel detail, northeast room, main block.

No more felicitous architectural style than the Federal can be encountered in North America. Neoclassical in form and spirit and derivative of the work of the English Adam brothers, particularly Robert, the Federal or Adamesque style became a fashionable mode of building in the 1780s, and its popularity continued until at least the 1820s. Charles Bulfinch of Boston is generally credited with having introduced the style to the United States in 1787. As with other "revivals" of the eighteenth and nineteenth centuries, the passion for neoclassical forms in decoration and building arrived in America after having been widely popularized in England. The progression from Georgian Palladian forms to the more chaste Adamesque was a natural one in the mercantile capitals of England. In America, where a war of independence was led by a merchant class seeking political *and* economic freedom, the spirit of the ancient republics was particularly welcomed. And in the hands of American architects and carpenter-builders from Maine to Georgia, the clean, stoic lines of classical inspiration replaced those of the more opulent, convoluted Georgian. The Federal may be considered America's first national style. It complements architecturally the decorative motifs and schemes adopted for coinage, emblems, and seals, and parallels the taste for simple classical elegance in furniture and clothing termed "Empire."

The "Federal," an American stylistic term reflective of the new republic, was a particularly appropriate one for public buildings—state houses, churches, custom houses, and other national governmental office buildings. Bulfinch selected it for the Massachusetts State House, and architects elsewhere—amateur or otherwise—followed his example. It was not long before home owners in small and large cities began building along neoclassical lines. Structures in what were then considered heavily populated areas—Boston, New York, Providence, Philadelphia—and in the South were generally built of brick. In Northern cities, disastrous fires in the eighteenth century had prompted the adoption of codes which prohibited the erection of wood structures. But in more rural areas of New England and of the Middle Atlantic states, the Federal style was often interpreted in wood. Perhaps nowhere is this more evident than in Salem, Massachusetts, where master woodcarver and architect Samuel McIntire created a virtual community of handsomely formed and embellished homes for the town's merchant class.

The bow-front town houses of Boston are the most obvious visual reminders of the Federal period in architecture. Although most houses in the style were squarish structures with little or no break in line, there was an attempt to relate external dimensions and internal spatial considerations. The use of bow-fronts, Venetian entrances with fan- and sidelights, and window recesses formed by semicircular relieving arches are all evidence of an aesthetic consideration for light and geometric form; room heights, of course, were much greater than those found in the typical Colonial of an earlier period. Windows, however, were generally of narrower dimensions than those found in Georgian buildings. Roofs were pitched at a lower angle and were not corniced as elaborately. On wooden structures, the boards were of a narrower variety than Colonial clapboard; on brick structures, a fine English bond rather than the Flemish was favored for many Georgian-style homes.

The Federal was the first of the American styles to be given popular attention through the printed word. This took the form of handbooks or builders' guides, the most famous of which was Asher Benjamin's *The American Builder's Companion*, first published in 1806. Benjamin was a follower of Bulfinch, and in 1803 listed himself in a Boston city directory as a "housewright." In the book, however, he terms himself an "Architect and Carpenter," and in every respect Benjamin was a professional. Through six editions, the last issued in 1826, he promulgated Adamesque principles of design. The book reflects a background in Georgian architecture and anticipates, particularly in the last edition, the coming of Greek Revival. But taken as a whole, it is about as coherent and as cogent a statement of a particular style as can be found in American architectural literature of the early nineteenth century. Benjamin was concerned with every aspect of the building, and includes in addition to basic information on the classical orders, designs for entrances, cornices, friezes, ornamental stucco ceilings, doors and sash, and windows.

Benjamin's principles of design and those of other Federal-style builders are outlined in a series of plans which are found in *The American Builder's Companion*. The plan and elevation for a small town house (Plate LI) is illustrated here. This is a four-story brick building of twelve rooms, excluding the kitchen and cellar floor. As noted, it is liberally supplied with fireplaces, central heating still being a dream of the future. The chimneys are positioned on the gable ends. The roof is low-pitched and is finished off by a simple entablature of brick with a projecting cornice. Windows are recessed on the main floor below semicircular arches and were probably intended to have double sash of six and six lights. The same arched treatment is given the front entrance, the space above undoubtedly intended to be fitted with a fanlight.

The two other Federal-style homes illustrated on the following pages are more ambitious designs. Both the Isaiah Davenport House (pp. 23-24) and the William Scarbrough House (pp. 25-27) are mansions. Each is located in Savannah, Georgia, and was completed between 1815 and 1820. These are dignified and sophisticated residences built for successful men of refinement and taste. Davenport was his own builder; Scarbrough engaged the architectural services of William Jay, an Englishman who settled in the Southeast in 1817 and was to remain there for seven years. What the two Savannah residences and Benjamin's design have in common are the graceful entryways, fanlights, arched windows, raised basements, and brick walls. The interior of the Benjamin town house presumably would have been finished in a less elegant manner than those of the two Savannah examples, but neoclassical designs for cornices, friezes, mantels, and ceiling ornaments in *The American Builder's Companion* suggest many common elements between the buildings. Arches, such as those at each end of the Davenport House living room (p. 24), were often incorporated in the design scheme. In the Scarbrough House, the end walls of the two parlors are gracefully curved, as are the windows at the opposite ends.

Each of the houses was built as a two- or two-and-a-half-story dwelling, the Scarbrough House having gained a third floor late in the 19th century which has since been removed. The rooms are large and clearly designed for entertaining as well as daily activity. First-floor ceilings are at least eleven feet high, creating an airy, classically proportioned setting. Utilitarian functions such as food preparation are consigned to the half-basement level. Open-well stairways were planned for each of the three houses. These beautifully curved stairways are economical in their use of space, yet endowed with aesthetic grace.

Small town house by Asher Benjamin from
The American Builder's Companion, 1811 (Pl. LI).

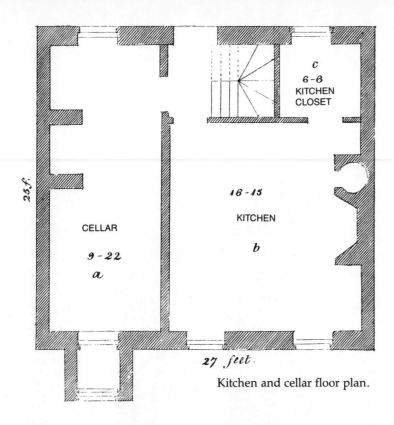

CELLAR

9 - 22

a

16 - 15

KITCHEN

b

c
6 - 8
KITCHEN
CLOSET

25 f.

27 feet.

Kitchen and cellar floor plan.

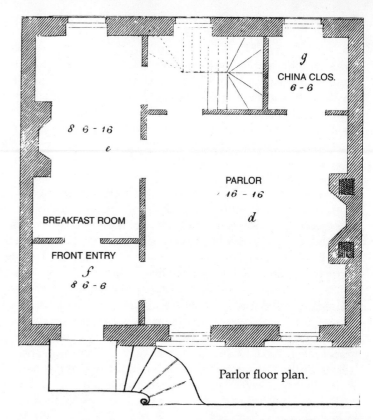

8 6 - 16

e

BREAKFAST ROOM

FRONT ENTRY

f
8 6 - 6

PARLOR
16 - 16

d

g
CHINA CLOS.
6 - 6

Parlor floor plan.

Chamber floor plan.

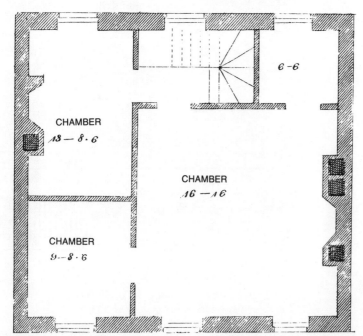

CHAMBER
13 — 8 · 6

CHAMBER
16 — 16

CHAMBER
9 — 8 · 6

6 - 6

Upper chamber floor plan.

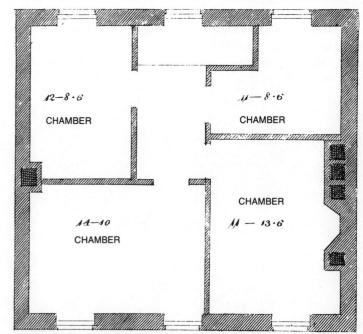

12 — 8 · 6

CHAMBER

11 — 8 · 6

CHAMBER

14 — 10

CHAMBER

11 — 13 · 6

CHAMBER

Isaiah Davenport House, Savannah, Georgia, 1815, south and east elevations.

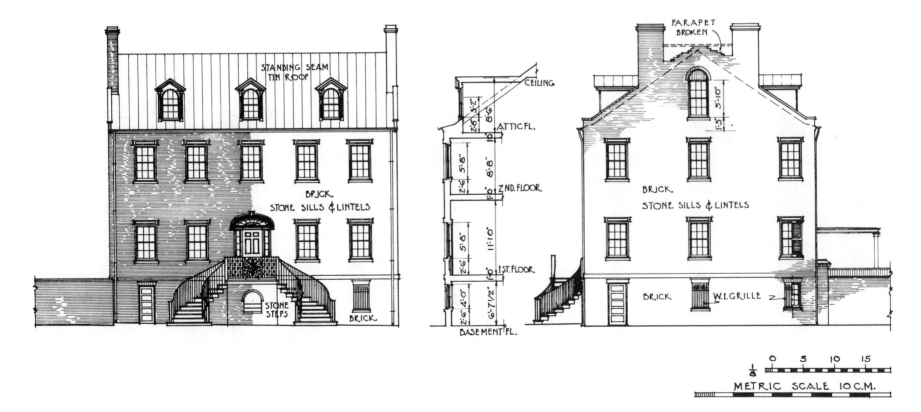

STANDING SEAM TIN ROOF

BRICK
STONE SILLS & LINTELS

STONE STEPS

BRICK

CEILING

3'-2"
2'-8"
8'-0"

ATTIC FL.

5'-8"
8'-8"
2'-6"
1'-0"

2ND. FLOOR

5'-8"
11'-10"
2'-6"
1'-0"

1ST. FLOOR

4'-0"
6'-7½"
2'-6"

BASEMENT FL.

PARAPET BROKEN

5'-10"
1'-5"

BRICK
STONE SILLS & LINTELS

BRICK   W.I. GRILLE

METRIC SCALE 10 C.M.

0   5   10   15
⅛

Detail, main doorway and entrance steps.

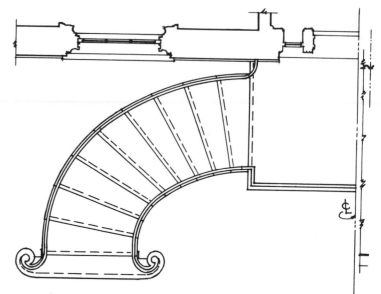

Elevation, main doorway and entrance steps.

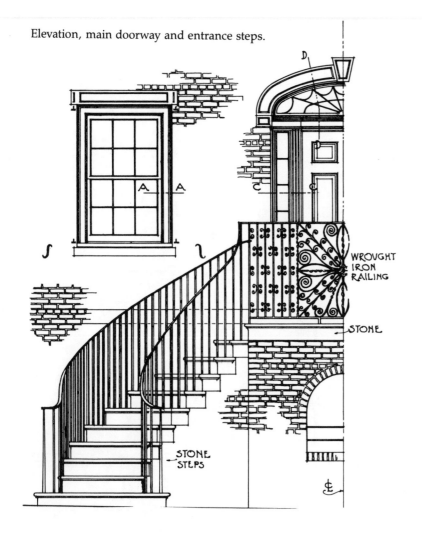

WROUGHT
IRON
RAILING

STONE

STONE
STEPS

Elevation, arch, living room, first
floor, north and south ends.

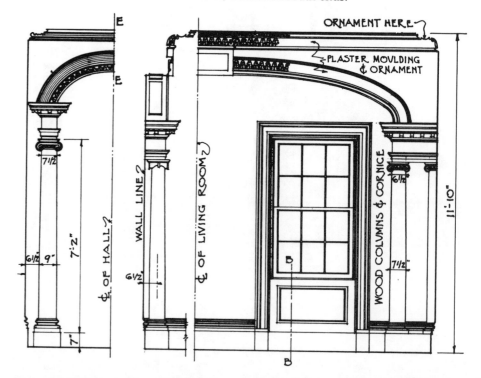

ORNAMENT HERE

PLASTER MOULDING
& ORNAMENT

WOOD COLUMNS & CORNICE

11'-10"

7½"

6½"

7½"

7'2"

9"

6½"

7"

6½"

℄ OF HALL

WALL LINE

℄ OF LIVING ROOM

E

E

B

B

Elevation, arch, hall, first floor.

ROOF RIDGE

THIRD FLOOR CEILING

THIRD FLOOR
SECOND FLOOR CEILING

SECOND FLOOR
FIRST FLOOR CEILING

FIRST FLOOR

William Scarbrough House, Savannah, Georgia, c. 1818-19,
c. 1834-45, William Jay, architect, east elevation.

First-floor plan.

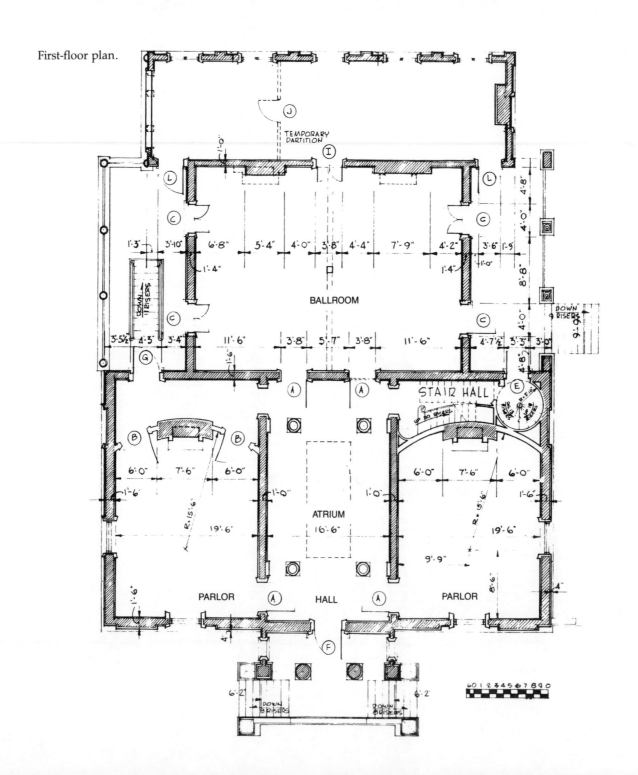

Second-floor plan.

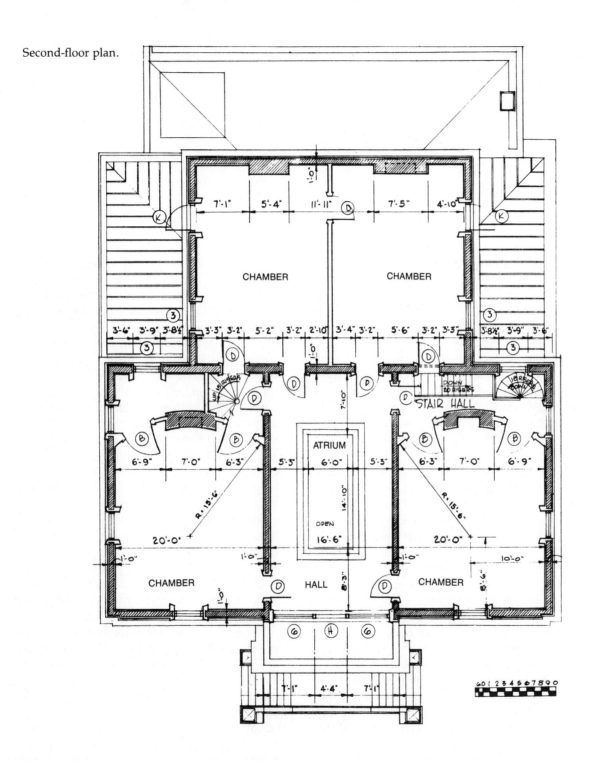

No two homes in America have been as celebrated and slavishly imitated as Washington's Mount Vernon and Scarlett O'Hara's Tara. Both are Southern plantation mansions which impress the viewer with a feeling of classical grandeur. Washington's country house, however, was but a rural villa until the addition of a two-story colonnaded porch and of wings at each end in 1784-85. It is the columned, neoclassical image of Mount Vernon which has been treasured by generations. In the late eighteenth century the orders of Roman and Greek architecture were avidly studied by architects and builders. From this time until the mid-nineteenth century, the neoclassical spirit in architecture swept from East to Far West, from Maine to the Deep South. Mount Vernon's grand colonnade was to serve as a model for similar piazzas or porches which dignified and romanticized the façades of such Greek Revival plantation homes as Tara and its real-life counterparts from the 1820s until the 1860s.

The first stage of the classical revival in the last years of the eighteenth century and first decade of the nineteenth was devoted primarily to the use of Roman models of Greek orders, particularly the Corinthian. Much of the public architecture of the period reflects a fascination with Roman monumentality that was particularly appropriate for "governmental" purposes. The simpler style of pure Greek origin, however, soon replaced that of the Roman, particularly in home building. The Greek temple form, albeit very formal, could be interpreted in modest ways, and the Ionic and Doric orders were the preferred modes throughout America. "The boldness of the Grecian Doric," Asher Benjamin wrote in 1827, "attracts the attention of the spectator by the grandeur and fine proportion of its parts, the form of its mouldings, and the beautiful variety of light and shade on their surfaces, which greatly relieves them from each other, and renders their contour distinct to the eye."

Guides to building in the Greek style were widely circulated throughout the land. Benjamin's *The Practice of Architecture* (1833) and *The Practical House Carpenter* (1830) went through many editions. The handbooks of Minard Lafever, *The Beauties of Modern Architecture* (1835) and *The Modern Builder's Guide* (1833), were also persuasive and useful compilations of designs. With such directions in hand, the reasonably skilled carpenter-builder in the Western Reserve of Ohio, the plains of Georgia, or other far-distant territories could fashion rather handsome one- or two-story homes.

The most typical of such structures are those which faithfully reproduce the temple façade, the round or square columns being constructed of wood, brick or stone. Those of the Doric order are simple fluted forms which are topped with a plain cushion capital, architrave, frieze panel, and cornice. The Ionic column is fitted in a capital with large volutes or spiral scrolls and ends in architrave, frieze, and cornice. The Corinthian column is the most elaborate and least encountered in American domestic building. The capital is shaped in the form of an inverted bell and contains volutes and two or three rows of acanthus leaves. The cornice and the rest of the entablature are richly ornamented.

Despite the availability of uniform specifications for such buildings, no two are exactly alike. Over time distinct variant forms developed regionally. In the North the columns were often tucked into the façade as pilasters. In the South the portico was deepened and sometimes even wrapped around three sides of the structure. A second-floor balcony with ornamental ironwork railings was often added across the front. Northern houses tended to be rather prim and proper; those of the South, more open and inviting.

Almost all Greek Revival residences do share some characteristic features. These include a low-pitched roof, frieze or pierced grille windows at what would be the attic level below the architrave band, cornices with dentils, Greek key fret ornamentation, broad architrave trim around doors and windows, and columned entryways with a rectangular transom and sidelights.

Greek Revival homes of all sorts reflect intelligent planning and sound aesthetic judgment often missing in domestic American architecture. If there is a fault to be found in the style, it is the lack of spontaneity which led to the encasing of home life in a strict structural framework. Such early critics of Greek Revival as Andrew Jackson Downing embraced instead a freer Gothic style. In their pursuit of the "picturesque," however, these champions of a new aesthetic failed to recognize the same qualities in many Greek Revival homes. Southerners were the last to give up their antebellum manners and modes. And "the more in ruin," Vincent Scully has commented, "the more Greek" their mansions seemed to be. If tragedy had been played out against a Northern backdrop, perhaps the neoclassical temples of good taste and propriety would have acquired a more tragic and therefore romantic image.

The Northern temple design is well illustrated in the Campbell-Whittlesey House (pp. 29-31), now handsomely restored as the home of the Landmark Society of Western New York. Although it cannot be attributed to Minard Lafever, the building greatly resembles the basic form he popularized both inside and out. The position of the great Ionic portico, however, is unlike many other examples of his work, for it does not frame the main entryway, but is found at the side. Behind the portico is a typical double parlor with windows that reach almost from floor to ceiling and fireplaces on the exterior walls of each room. The building is divided functionally into two sections: a square temple front portion with a grand spiral stairway and entry hall, library, and the parlors; and a rectangular rear portion containing dining and breakfast rooms and service areas. Typically, the kitchen is found on the first floor and not in the basement, as was often the case with earlier architectural styles.

Like the Campbell-Whittlesey House, the Skinner-Trowbridge residence (pp. 31-33) has a grand Ionic portico which fronts the formal reception rooms. The architect, Ithiel Town, made dramatic use of a large bay window in the dining room, a feature that would be incorporated in many slightly later Gothic Revival and Italianate-style houses.

The James F. D. Lanier Home (pp. 34-39), designed by Francis Costigan, illustrates just how imaginatively the Greek Revival style evolved. The two-and-a-half story brick building little resembles the classical temples of old. The wood Corinthian columns form a platform for the architrave, a frieze embellished with wreaths, an elaborate cornice, a crown decorated with an anthemion ornament, and, finally, a decorative stucco and wood cupola. The same ornamental details are to be found on the west elevation, and here the Doric columns are part of the side walls, projecting slightly *in antis.* On the east side of the main block is a one-and-a-half story ell which, as the floor plan indicates (p. 39), houses the kitchen and service area.

The interior plan of the Lanier Home is rigorously symmetrical and formal with the exception of the dramatic three-story spiral staircase (p. 38). It rises in the center of the house and ends in an eight-sided tower with skylight.

The two Southern Greek Revival homes shown—the René Beauregard House (p. 34) and the Andrews-Taylor House (pp. 40-44)—share Doric porticoes, rather than the more common Ionic form found in the North, and make effective use of outdoor balconies. Both are plantation or farm residences, the Beauregard house being distinguished by what might be called its full-length "Mt. Vernon" portico and low hip roof. The Andrews-Taylor residence, Lady Bird Johnson's birthplace and childhood home, is only one room deep and, as was long a practice in the South, includes a first-floor bedroom.

Campbell-Whittlesey House, Rochester, New York, 1835-36, architect unknown, north elevation.

First-floor *(left)* and second-floor *(right)* plans.

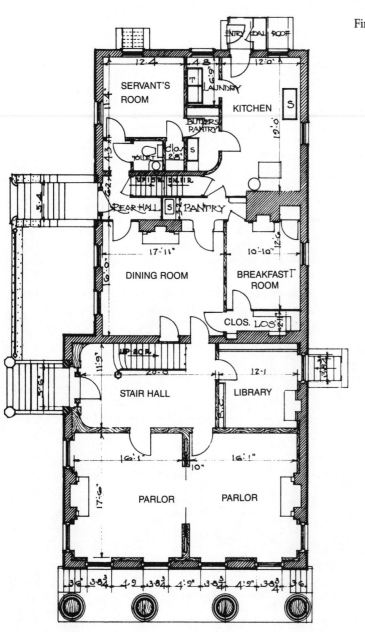

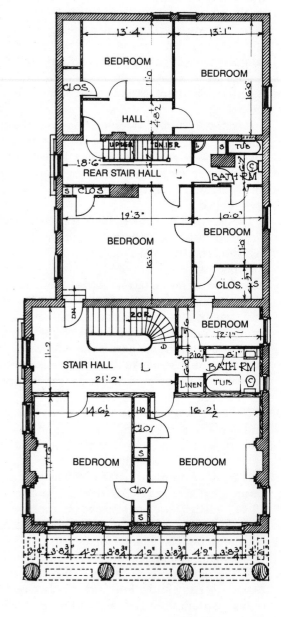

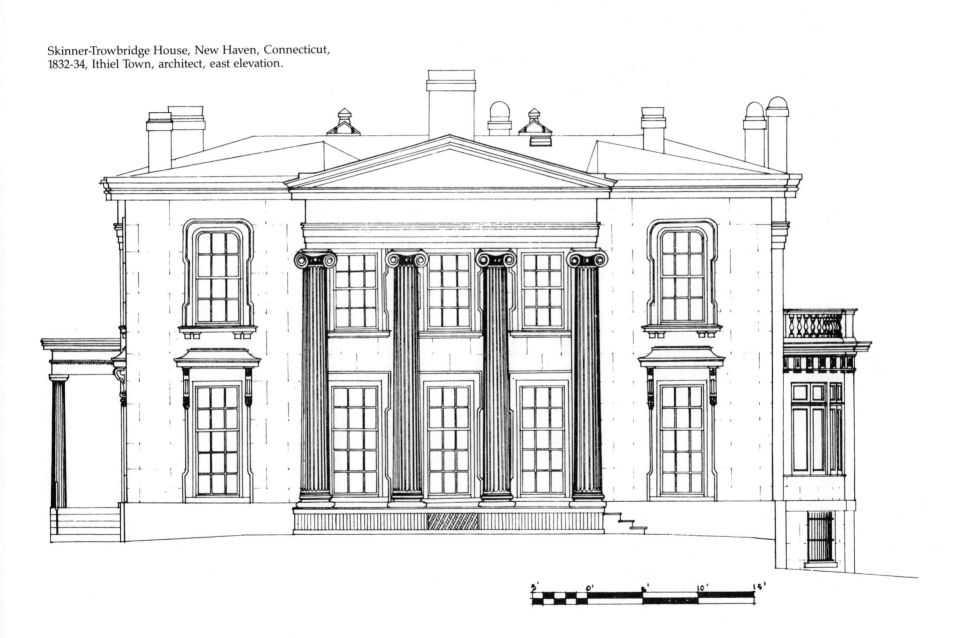

Skinner-Trowbridge House, New Haven, Connecticut, 1832-34, Ithiel Town, architect, east elevation.

First-floor plan.

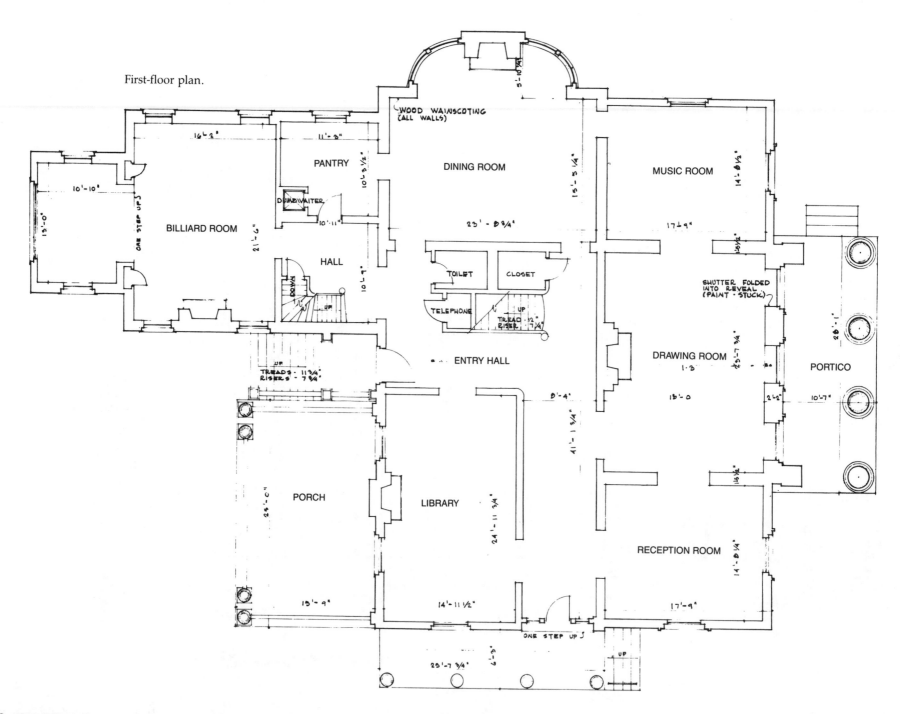

WOOD WAINSCOTING
(ALL WALLS)

16'-2"   11'-2"

PANTRY   DINING ROOM   MUSIC ROOM

10'-10"   10'-3 1/2"   14'-0 1/2"

15'-0"   DUMBWAITER   15'-5 1/4"   17'-9"

BILLIARD ROOM   10'-11"

21'-6"   15 1/2"

ONE STEP UP   10'-1"   HALL   23'-0 3/4"

DOWN   TOILET   CLOSET   SHUTTER FOLDED
INTO REVEAL
(PAINT - STUCK)

UP   TELEPHONE   25'-7 3/4"

ENTRY HALL   UP
TREAD - 12"
RISER - 7 1/4"   DRAWING ROOM   20'-1"

UP   1-3   PORTICO
TREADS - 11 3/4"
RISERS - 7 3/4"   13'-0

8'-4"   2 1/2"   10'-7"

41'-1 3/4"   15 1/2"

25'-0"   PORCH   LIBRARY   RECEPTION ROOM   14'-0 1/4"

24'-11 3/4"

15'-9"   14'-11 1/2"   17'-9"

ONE STEP UP   6'-3"

UP

23'-7 3/4"

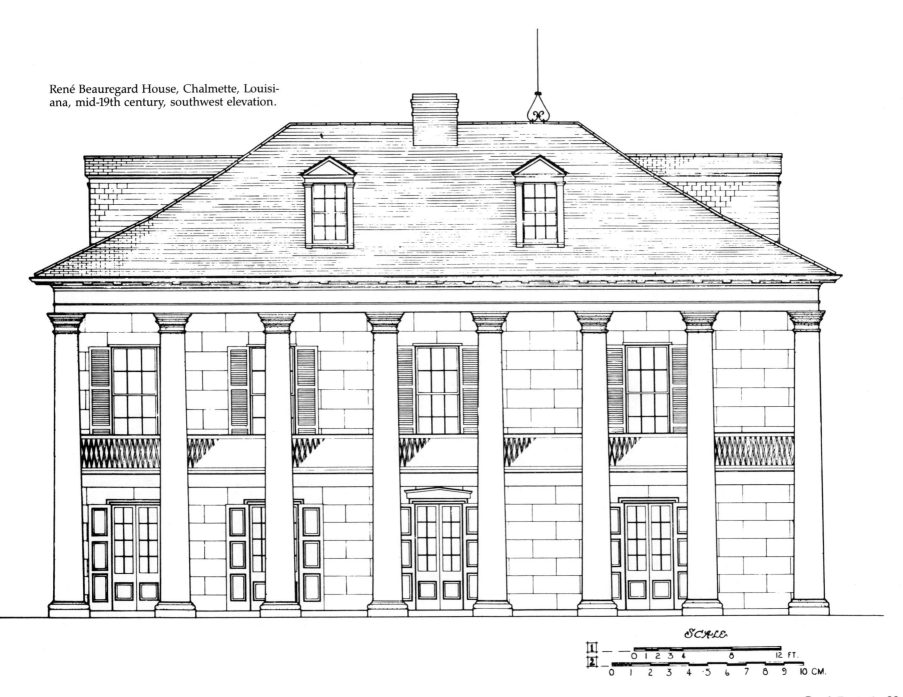

René Beauregard House, Chalmette, Louisiana, mid-19th century, southwest elevation.

SCALE

James F. D. Lanier Home, Madison, Indiana, 1840-44,
Francis Costigan, architect, south elevation.

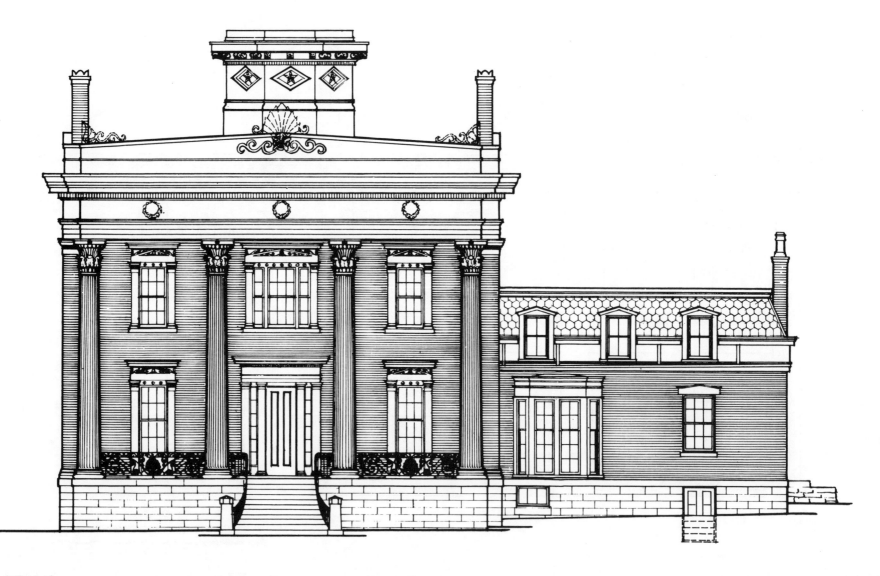

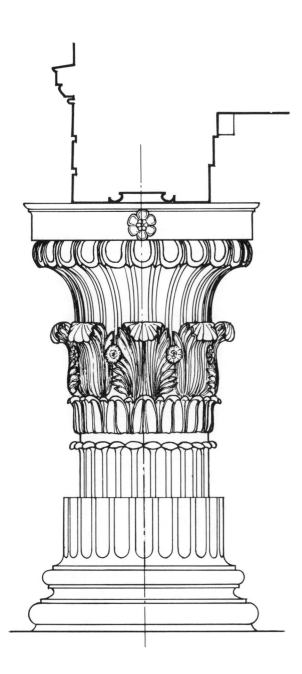

Portico column, rail, and steps details.

SCALE

West elevation.

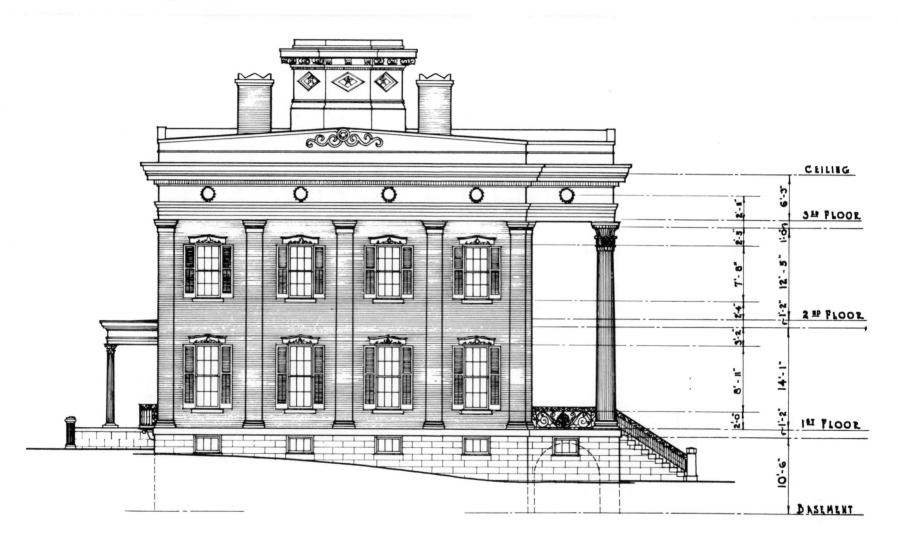

CEILING

6'-3" 2'-1"

3ᴿᴰ FLOOR

1'-0" 2'-5"

7'-8" 12'-5"

2ᴺᴰ FLOOR 6'-2" 2'-4"

3'-2"

8'-11" 14'-1"

1ˢᵀ FLOOR 6'-2" 2'-0"

10'-6"

BASEMENT

Transverse section

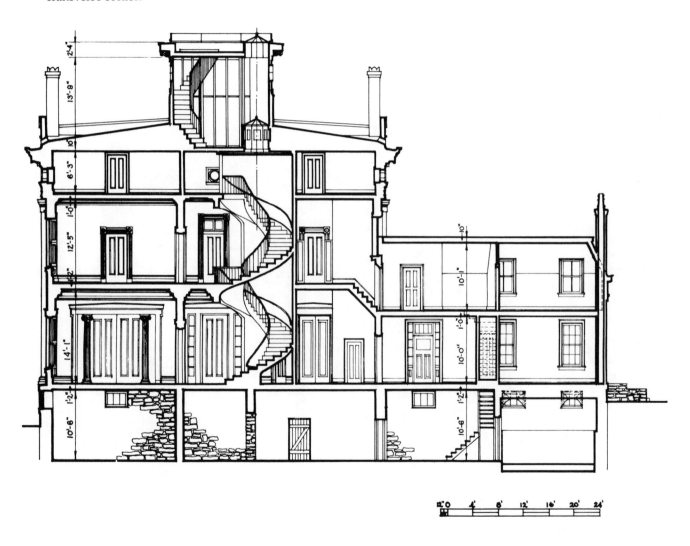

Stair elevation.

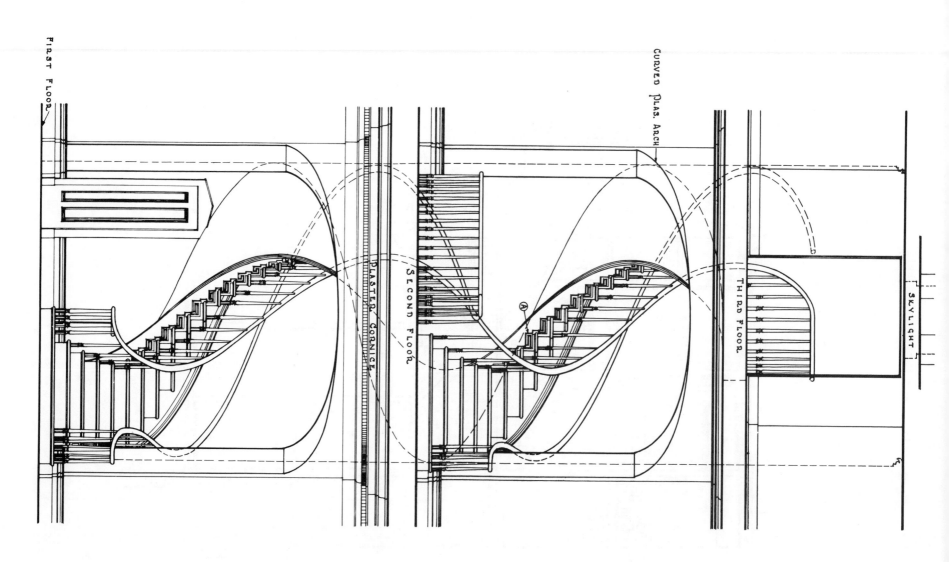

First-floor plan.

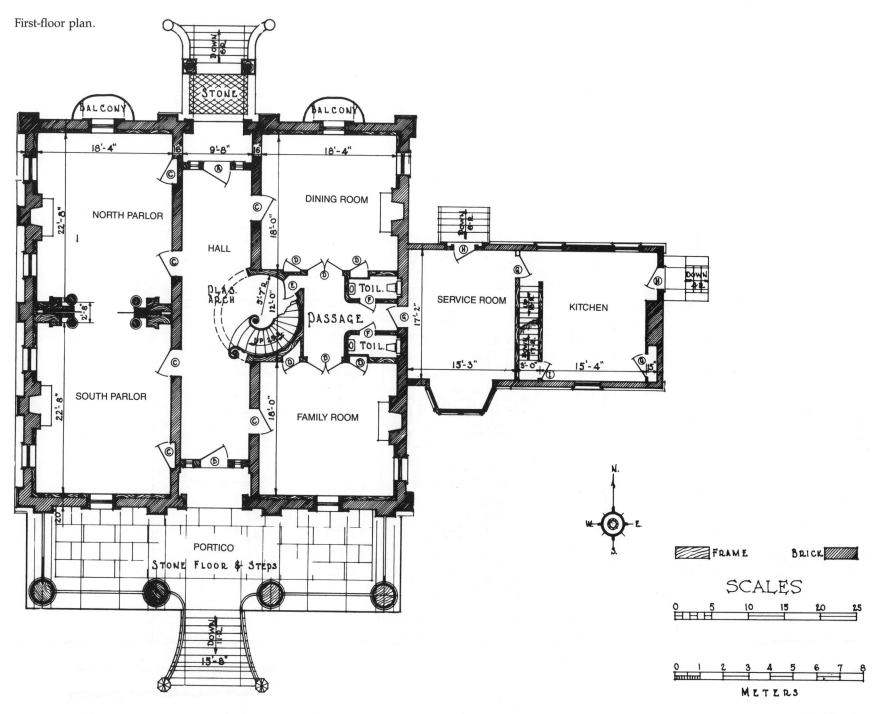

STONE

BALCONY   BALCONY

18'-4"   16   9'-8"   16   18'-4"

C   A

NORTH PARLOR   C   DINING ROOM

22'-8"

HALL   18'-0"   H

DOWN 6 R.

D   D

PLAS.
ARCH   E   D   Toil.   SERVICE ROOM   KITCHEN

5'-7R.   F   DOWN
4 R.

2'-8"   12'-0"   PASSAGE   G   17'-2"   UP 17 R.   DOWN 17 R.

UP 15 R.   D   F   Toil.   15'-3"   3'-0"   15'-4"   15

22'-8"   C

SOUTH PARLOR   D   D   T

FAMILY ROOM   18'-0"

C

C   D

20   N.

PORTICO   W.   E.
STONE FLOOR & STEPS

S.

DOWN 11 R.

15'-8"

FRAME   BRICK

SCALES

0   5   10   15   20   25

0   1   2   3   4   5   6   7   8

METERS

Andrews-Taylor House, Karnack vicinity, Texas, 1843, west
elevation.

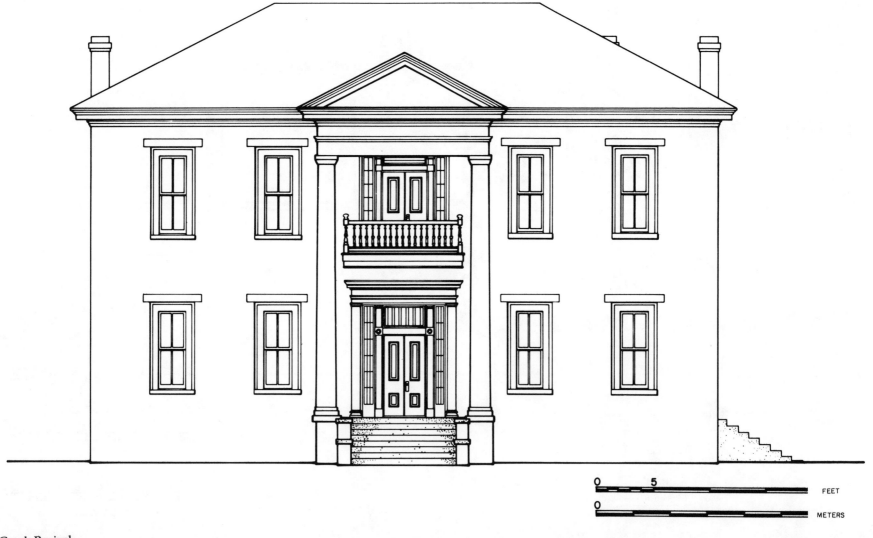

0   5

FEET

0

METERS

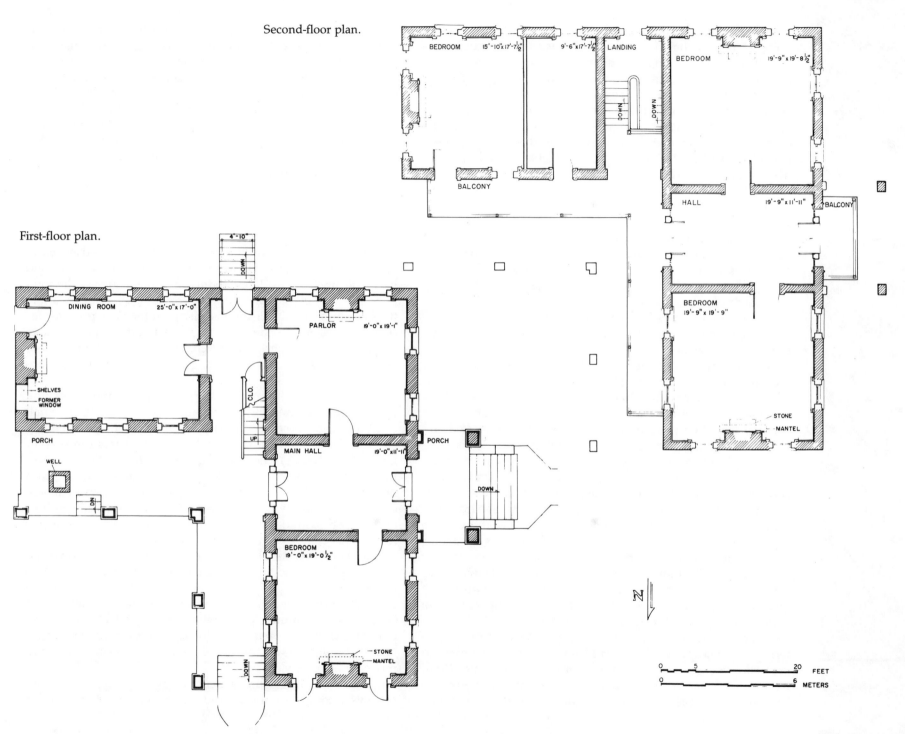

Second-floor plan.

BEDROOM 15'-10"x17'-7½" 9'-6"x17'-7½" LANDING BEDROOM 19'-9" x 19'-8½"

DOWN DOWN

BALCONY

HALL 19'-9"x11'-11" BALCONY

First-floor plan.

4'-10"

DOWN

DINING ROOM 25'-0"x 17'-0"

PARLOR 19'-0"x 19'-1"

BEDROOM 19'-9" x 19'-9"

SHELVES

FORMER
WINDOW

CLO.

UP

PORCH MAIN HALL 19'-0"x11'-11" PORCH

WELL

DOWN

UP

STONE
MANTEL

BEDROOM
19'-0"x 19'-0½"

DOWN

STONE
MANTEL

N

0   5   20 FEET
0   6 METERS

The cottage enjoyed a popularity in the New World far beyond that achieved in rural England. Often defined as a "small rustic" structure, this kind of building served the needs of many social classes, including workmen and country gentlemen. Despite popular misconception, a cottage can be a quite large, imposing structure, as were many built in North America and Great Britain during the first half of the nineteenth century. In general, however, this type of house was built on a small scale. As conceived by Andrew Jackson Downing, Andrew Jackson Davis, and Richard Upjohn, it was designed in the Gothic style, and expressed much in the way of romantic "feeling," to use one of Downing's favorite terms. "Now, every cottage may not display *science* or knowledge," he wrote in *The Architecture of Country Houses* (1850), "because science demands architectural education in its builder or designer, as well as, in many cases, some additional expense. But *feeling* may be evinced by every one possessing it. . . . " The Gothic-style cottage in America was a simple, democratic, and pleasantly liveable building form that suited the needs of a people seeking a change from the formal and aristocratic Federal and Greek Revival styles.

Simple domestic dwellings such as the Downing cottage illustrated here (p. 46) are often termed "Carpenter Gothic." Most are the work of carpenter/builders and not architects. Almost all display the kind of fancy woodwork which we automatically call "gingerbread"—finials, verge or bargeboards, brackets, canopies, For Downing, however, the terms "Carpenter Gothic" and "gingerbread" were anathematic. The architectural elements which he suggested provided "feeling," a "softening and humanizing expression," and were of the hand and not the machine-made sort. "All ornaments which are not simple," Downing wrote, "and cannot be executed in a substantial and appropriate manner, should at once be rejected; all flimsy and meager decorations which have a pasteboard effect, are as unworthy of, and unbecoming for the house of him who understands the true beauty of a cottage life, as glass breastpins or gilt-pewter spoons would be for his personal ornaments or family service of plate." Unfortunately, not all followers of Downing (or the many other exponents of the cottage style) shared his love of quality and appropriateness. They were, however, unanimous in their appreciation of the outlines of the new style.

Cottages in the Downing style, many copied directly from his pattern books, first appeared in the Hudson Valley and Northeast and gradually emerged as far west as California in prefabricated form. Design II, a "small bracketed cottage," is one of the simplest of the Downing forms to be presented in *The Architecture of Country Houses*.

It displays many of the very basic elements of country Gothic design—the use of vertical board walls, a steep gable roof, diamond-paned sashes, a bay window, handsomely finished chimney tops, and brackets over windows and doors. Downing felt that vergeboards were appropriate only for a villa, but he did use them in fancier cottage designs. "A bay window," he wrote, "does not of necessity belong to a small cottage [but it] raises the character of such a cottage wherever it is simple and tastefully introduced."

The inner spaces are arranged in as workable and attractive a manner as is possible in a modest home. The living room is clearly separated from the other ground-floor rooms and is provided with a pleasant bay-window nook, a fireplace, and two ample closets on each side of the fireplace. This room is designed as a proper parlor. "The real living room of the family," Downing explained, "will, in great measure, be also the kitchen . . . ; [it] will be used as a back-kitchen for the rough-work, washing, etc., so that in summer, and indeed at any time, the living room can be made to have the comfortable aspect of a cottage parlor by confining the rough-work to the kitchen proper." A lean-to addition on the back provides for storage of coal on one side and a pantry on the other with a separate outside kitchen entrance in between. The second or chamber floor is neatly divided into three sleeping areas, two of which are supplied with flues for stove pipes.

The A. B. Austin House (pp. 43-45) is typical of farmhouses built in the Gothic Revival style throughout the country in the first half of the nineteenth century. The vertical board and batten wood siding covering three-quarters of the building emphasizes the upward thrust of the style. As when viewing a Gothic church, the eye moves up rather than across the building. The gables trimmed with decorative vergeboards give further emphasis to the upward dimension. This verticality is also expressed in the east façade with its decorative balustraded entry porch and the arched doorway above it.

The other architectural appointments are more regular and could just as well be found on a boxy Greek Revival- or Italianate-style house of the same period. Few mid- to late-nineteenth-century American homes are stylistically pure in every respect; rather, they borrow motifs common to several different architectural schools, one of these usually predominating, as is the case with the Austin house. The windows and doors, for example, are designed in a common vernacular style.

In floor plan, the Austin residence breaks down into three components: a long vertical main section containing a double parlor and entry hall in the front; an ell behind for the dining room, bedroom, and washroom; and a one-story kitchen-service wing (probably added later). The second floor, extending across the first two sections, contains a hall, three bedrooms, and storage space.

Architectural critics today loudly lament the lack of well-designed plans for modest homes, and they are right. The characterless boxes which pass for places of repose are a far cry from those picturesque cottages with "feeling" popularized by Downing and his contemporaries. The small, romantic Gothic touches added to these buildings immeasurably increased their personal and real value.

A. B. Austin House, Paris, Illinois, 1844-45, east entrance and porch detail.

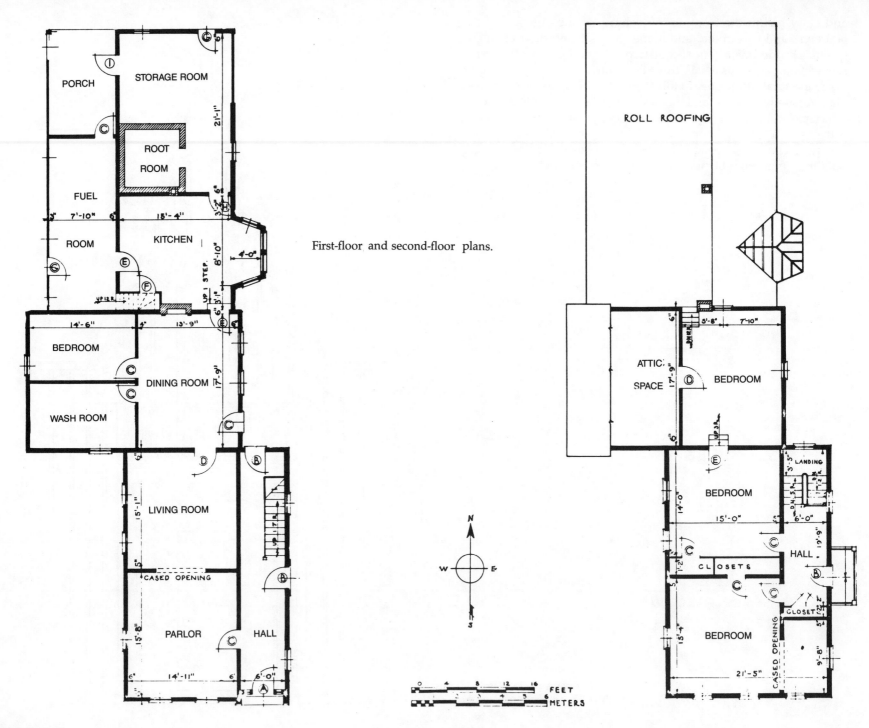

First-floor and second-floor plans.

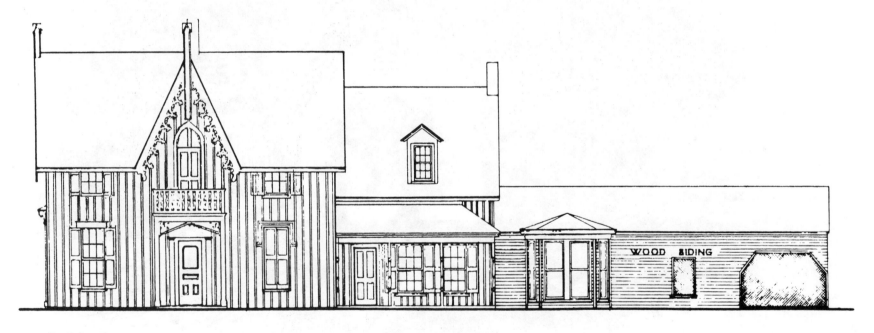

East elevation.

Small bracketed cottage by Andrew Jackson Downing from
The Architecture of Country Houses, 1850 (Design II).

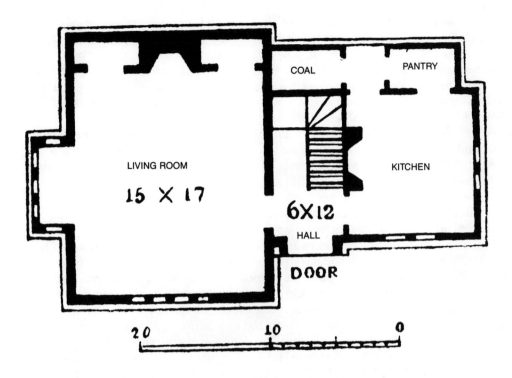

LIVING ROOM

15 × 17

COAL

PANTRY

KITCHEN

6×12

HALL

DOOR

20   10   0

First-floor and second-floor plans.

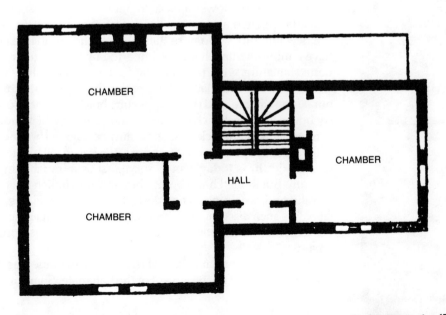

CHAMBER

CHAMBER

CHAMBER

HALL

No term can adequately describe the American fashion for the classical and picturesque in architecture and landscaping during the mid-nineteenth century. "The Italianate" is as broad a term as can be applied to the romantic style of a non-Gothic sort which appeared first in the Northeast. Some have called it Tuscan; others, Anglo-Italian. Architect John Notman's 1837 house for Bishop Doane at Burlington, New Jersey, was, to all intents, an Italian villa not unlike those found in the Tuscan countryside. Andrew Jackson Downing popularized Notman's design and those of Andrew Jackson Davis in two books of the period, *Cottage Residences* (1842) and *The Architecture of Country Houses* (1850). Other architects such as William H. Ranlett also sought to spread the word of the new style which had first gained popularity in England. In volume II of his series of designs (1851), Ranlett argues that the Anglo-Italian "might with greater propriety be called the American-Italian, for it is more purely American than Italian in character, and hardly at all resembles the English style of villas." Although relatively faithful to European models, even the first Italianate houses built for innovative and wealthy clients lacked the elaborate decoration and appointments of the Old World. Such "richness," according to Ranlett, "would ill accord with the severity of our republican habits, and that predominance of economy and comfort which so distinctly mark all the efforts of American art."

The American structure was distinguished primarily by the use of projecting eaves and heavy supporting brackets. By no means was campanile or tower a basic ingredient in the design. Again, Ranlett explained and rationalized away the differences between the new and old: "The pure Italian villas and palatial residences have a monumental character, imparted by their regular proportioned tablature, which our so-called Anglo-Italian villas with their bracketed eaves must lack. These projecting eaves, so becoming in our sunny climate, and their supporting brackets impart to a country house an aspect of cheerfulness and comfort which more than compensates for the lack of classic beauty occasioned by the absence of the regularly proportioned cornice of the Italian villa." Such eaves, one would think today, would serve just as admirably in sunny Tuscany. But Ranlett had a point: the American Italianate style was as valid and becoming as any derivative fashion could be. By the late 1850s such discussions of stylistic purity were largely academic; the general public knew only of houses in the "Italian order" or "manner."

The basic rectangular profile of the American home was not appreciably changed by the advent of the Italianate. Some of the early designs make use of an "L"-shaped floor plan; others employ the "T." Later homes were more likely to assume a standard box-like shape. Almost all, however, make use of broad eaves and brackets, the latter often found in pairs. The roofs are generally of the low hip variety and slope very gently. Windows are much narrower than those found in houses of an earlier style and are often paired or even grouped in threes. Some windows are circular-headed. A three-story tower or campanile might be found angled at a corner of the structure or set to one side of the main part of the façade. The use of the balcony, veranda loggia, cupola, and belvidere and bay windows further accentuates the picturesque qualities of an Italianate house.

A study of elevations and floor plans will suggest something of an architect's intention to introduce interest in a house by incorporating balconies and a veranda. This was also accomplished by placing such major structural forms as a tower at an arresting angle to the main house. As historian Vincent Scully has noted, "Picturesque buildings were meant to unfold to the viewer over time, as he approached them along the contrived curves of their site plans or, inside, wandered from room to room according to an asymmetrical pattern which created the effect of freedom and discovery." This sense of the unusual and expansive would have been experienced by a visitor to the Morse-Libby House (pp. 49-51), designed by one of America's great architects, Henry Austin.

The brownstone home, also known as the Victoria Mansion, was built for R. S. Morse, a wealthy New Orleans hotel owner. No building could have been more stylish—inside or out—for its time. Architectural historians would describe the late 1850s building as an example of the Italian Villa rather than the Italianate style in order to differentiate between Austin's complex assymetrical structure with its imposing tower and the more typical, somewhat later (1860s) bracketed box. Austin also designed homes in the simpler Italianate style (pp. 52-53). This distinction, however, is academic, for both types of buildings incorporate similar elements popular during the mid-Victorian period.

The tower of the Austin mansion is only slightly off-center. The impression of greater irregularity is created primarily by the projecting pavilion to its right, a handsome neoclassical architectural counterpoint. It is as if Austin moved the traditional central pavilion of a Georgian Colonial residence to one side in order to fit the bell tower. Other details, however, suggest that his design was not merely a reworking of old ideas. Although there are rigorously classical pedimented windows in the second story of the tower and pavilion, the majority of the openings, including the main entrance, are round-headed. In addition, the architect has gracefully interwoven a balcony, loggia, and veranda to unify the various elements.

In floor plan, the Morse-Libby House conforms to its façade; the tower shelters a vestibule on the first floor, an imaginative sitting room on the second or bedroom floor, and a stairwell on the third. As is common in other Italianate houses, a wide center hall contains the main stairway and access to rooms on each side. The Morse-Libby House, however, is much larger than other homes of the same style. The additional space makes possible amenities such as a music room, library, billiard room, six bedrooms, and a generously proportioned parlor (35 feet long and 25 feet wide).

The Willis Bristol House (pp. 52-53) is a more typical Italianate design, making use of a straightforward rectangular form, cornice brackets, balconies, and a bay window. In architect Austin's hands, however, it assumed imaginative dimensions and details which make it distinctive. The elaborate door and window fenestration, ornate ironwork, and fanciful entry porch imbue the structure with an exotic, romantic feeling.

The Austin, Texas, residence (pp. 54-57) is a superb example of a modest yet stylish Italianate residence. Its single story contains a center hall and five well-proportioned rooms in the center block. The bracketed cornice, ornamental porch, and rounded windows are perfectly balanced. Note that the sash are simply two over two rather than the six over six common to earlier examples. Most Italianate houses of the period would not have included such fine details as cut stone for the corner blocks or quoins and for the window trim; they would have been built entirely of wood.

All of the examples shown on these pages are built on half basements and have wide hip roofs which are crowned in some fashion. Although differing greatly in other design elements, each is extraordinarily appealing in its arrangement of picturesque details, a hallmark of the best in Italianate design.

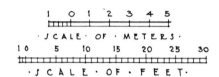

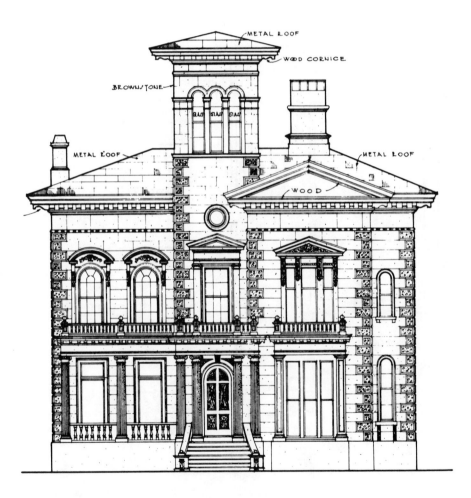

Morse-Libby House, Portland, Maine, 1859-63, Henry Austin, architect, front elevation.

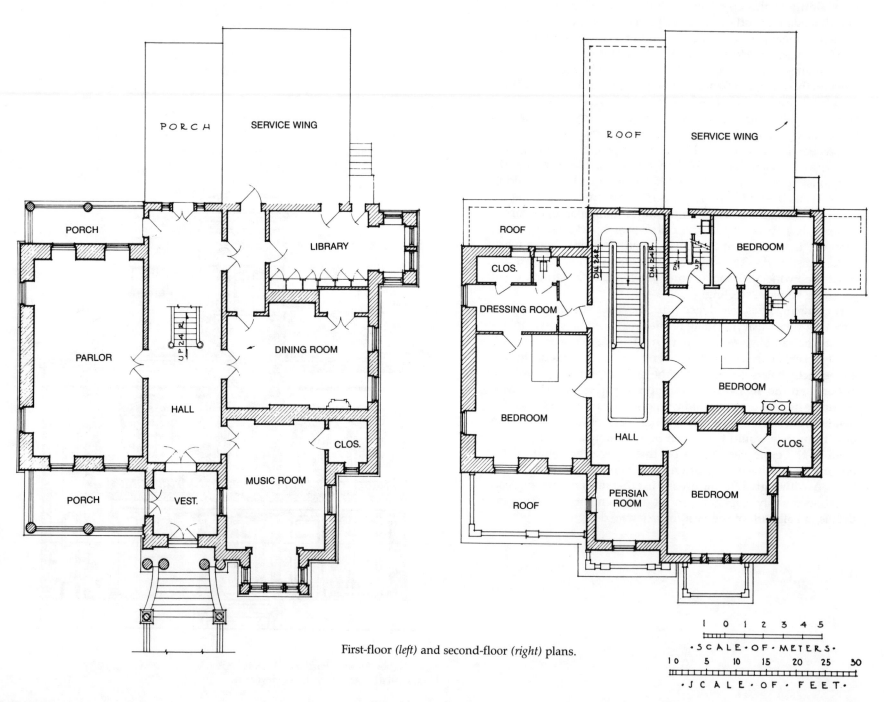

PORCH

SERVICE WING

PORCH

LIBRARY

PARLOR

UP 24 R.

DINING ROOM

HALL

CLOS.

PORCH

VEST.

MUSIC ROOM

ROOF

SERVICE WING

ROOF

CLOS.

BEDROOM

DRESSING ROOM

DN. 24 R.

DN. 24 R.

UP

BEDROOM

BEDROOM

BEDROOM

HALL

CLOS.

ROOF

PERSIAN ROOM

BEDROOM

First-floor *(left)* and second-floor *(right)* plans.

1 0 1 2 3 4 5
·SCALE·OF·METERS·

10   5   10   15   20   25   30
·SCALE·OF·FEET·

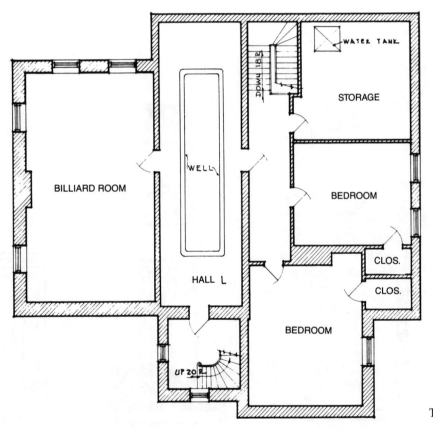

WATER TANK

STORAGE

DOWN 18 R.

WELL

BILLIARD ROOM

BEDROOM

CLOS.

CLOS.

HALL L

BEDROOM

UP 20 R.

Third-floor plan.

Willis Bristol House, New Haven, Connecticut,
1846, Henry Austin, architect, north elevation.

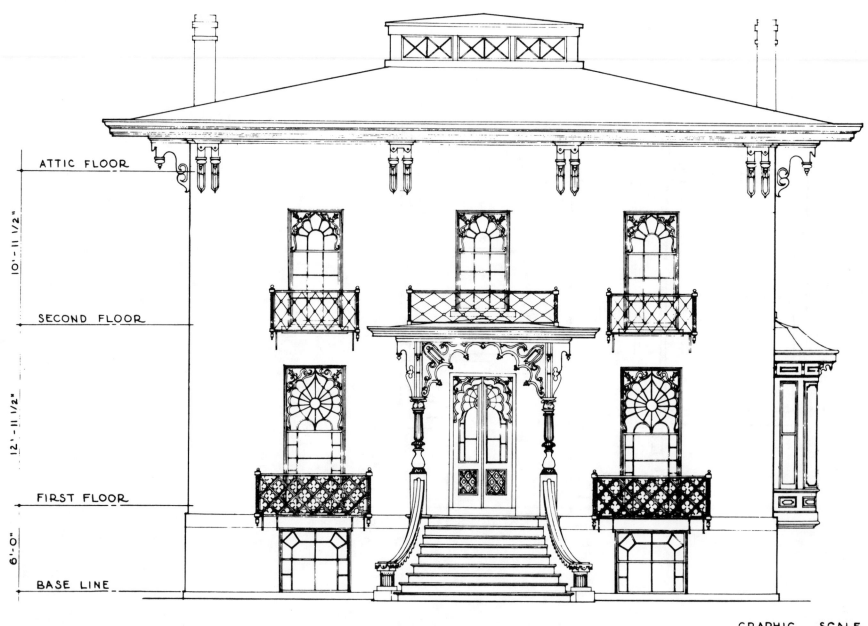

ATTIC FLOOR

10' - 11 1/2"

SECOND FLOOR

12' - 11 1/2"

FIRST FLOOR

6' - 0"

BASE LINE

GRAPHIC SCALE
1' 0   2'   4'   6' 8'

First-floor plan.

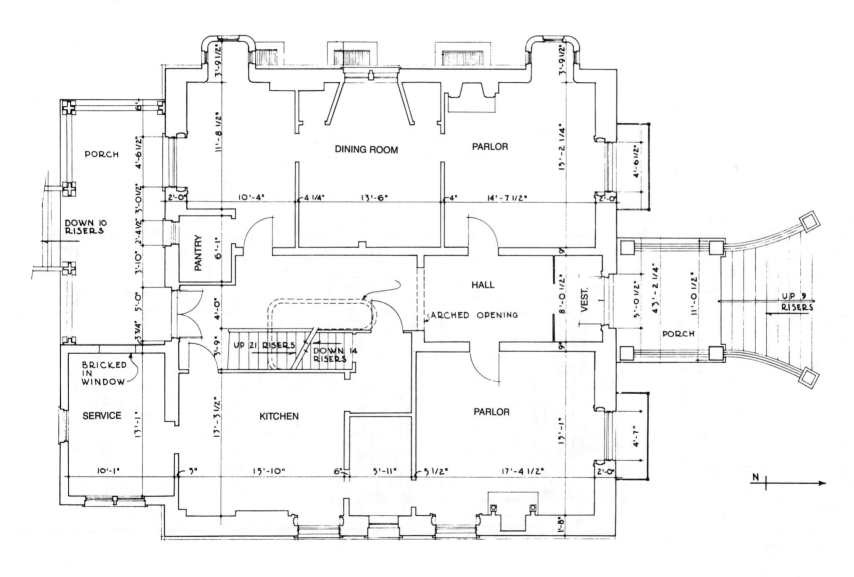

PORCH

DOWN 10
RISERS

PANTRY

BRICKED
IN
WINDOW

SERVICE

DINING ROOM

PARLOR

HALL

ARCHED OPENING

UP 21 RISERS

DOWN 14
RISERS

KITCHEN

PARLOR

VEST.

PORCH

UP 9
RISERS

N

Residence, Austin, Texas, late 19th century, south elevation.

South window and main entrance doorway details with molding profiles.

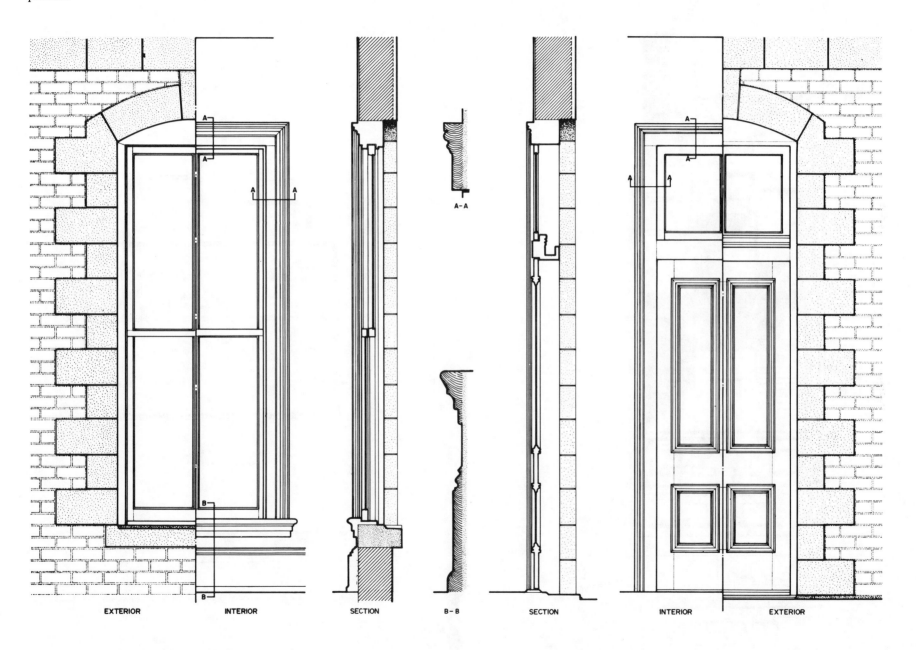

EXTERIOR INTERIOR SECTION B-B SECTION INTERIOR EXTERIOR

A-A

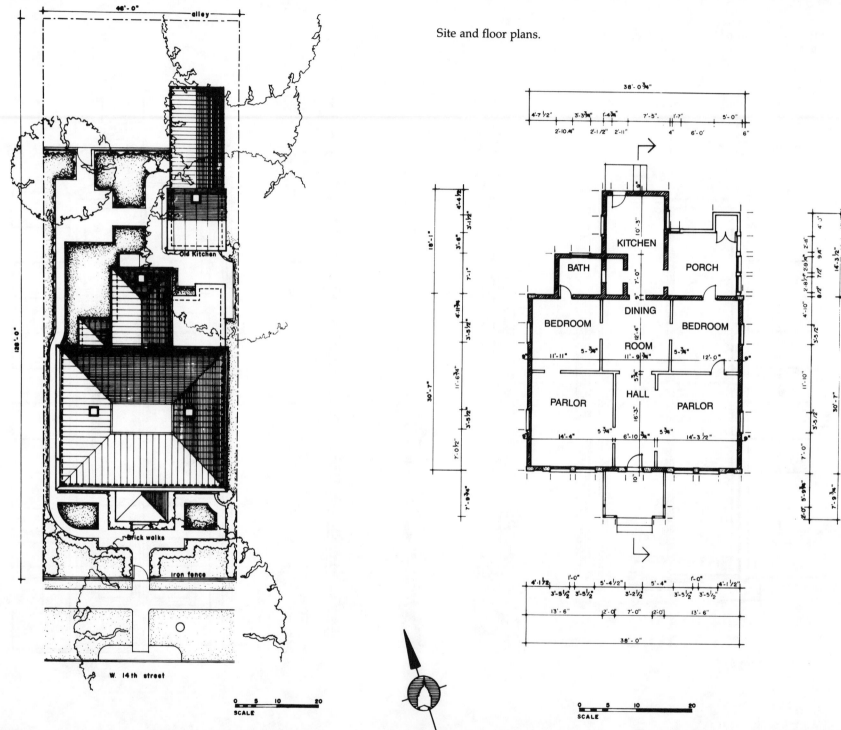

Site and floor plans.

KITCHEN

BATH

PORCH

DINING

BEDROOM

BEDROOM

ROOM

PARLOR

HALL

PARLOR

SCALE

0 5 10 20

Sectional view.

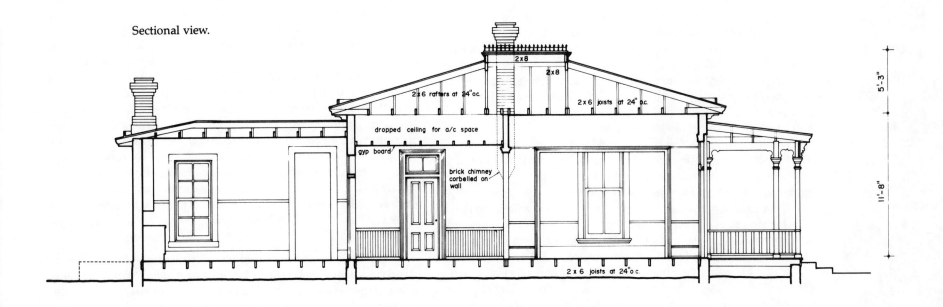

2 x 8
2 x 8

2 x 6 rafters at 24" o.c.
2 x 6 joists at 24" o.c.

dropped ceiling for a/c space

gyp board

brick chimney
corbelled on
wall

2 x 6 joists at 24" o.c.

5'-3"

11'-8"

0 1   3   5   10
SCALE IN FEET

Homes in this style popular during the years from 1860 to 1880 have won renewed appreciation only recently. Indubitably Victorian, such structures suggest much that was overstuffed and mannered in the mid- to late-nineteenth century. The Mansard style has also been called the General Grant style, a not unfitting designation for an architectural form which suited the needs of the bourgeoisie of the Gilded Age. The felicities of the Mansard style are not to be found in scale or ornament. These were somewhat top-heavy, lumbering structures. What then is there to celebrate? A great number of such buildings—public and domestic—exhibit a refreshing degree of imaginative eclecticism. The juxtaposition of a towering center pavilion against the mass of the mansarded structure, the use of sweeping porches or piazzas, the generous display of various building materials such as slate, tin and wood—these elements are worthy of study and preservation. Such features are exhibited in the modest homes illustrated here, and in such nationally-acclaimed civic structures as the Boston City Hall, Philadelphia's City Hall, and the Executive Office Building in Washington, D.C.

Directly or indirectly, American architects were influenced by the design of the extension to the Louvre in Paris (1852-57). The central architectural landmark of the Second Empire of Napoleon III, it was first copied in England as a fitting model for monumental public buildings. The first Grand Central Depot in New York (1869-71), designed by Isaac C. Buckhout and J. B. Snook, was a splendid palace in the Mansard mode with three square-domed pavilions, and the New Louvre was its inspiration.

It was long thought that the term "Mansard" owed its origin to the French architect François Mansart (1598-1666), the original designer of the Louvre, but this attribution is questioned today. The word "mansarde" in French, however, does mean a garret or attic and there can be no mistaking the style of a house with a top floor which is described in French as *mansardé*. Adoption of the mansard was not merely a stylistic gesture but was, as well, a utilitarian improvement: the pitch of the average mansard roof allows for greater use of attic space for living purposes. The slope of nearly every mansard roof, of course, is broken by dormer windows. The slope of the roof varies greatly from building to building. The majority form straight angles, but others curve convexly or concavely. In almost every case, the roof is clearly delineated from the mass of the building by a bracketed cornice. Chimneys are given considerable prominence and are often capped in a highly ornamental fashion. Windows, too, are frequently given decorative relief in the form of curved heads described as "eye-brow." The windows may be curved or rectilinear, and are often paired.

Buildings in the Second Empire style were especially popular in small and large cities from the 1860s through the '80s. A considerable number of these dwellings survive today in Northern and Western manufacturing centers. Ironically, the mansard roof has often been removed or covered over, thus destroying not only the aesthetic appeal of the building but, to some extent, its very utility. The Second Empire is essentially a vertical style, unlike the horizontal Greek Revival or Italianate. By making maximum use of attic and/or second-floor space with a mansard roof and dormers, an amazing number of rooms could be fitted into a narrow building on a small lot. At a time when urban property was becoming more expensive and scarce, building "up" rather than across a lot made perfectly good economic sense.

The utilitarian and aesthetic properties of the Mansard style were also recognized in less congested areas. Any number of older Colonial-style houses were fitted out with a new mansard roof line; it is not unusual to encounter such stylistic hybrids today. The economy of this building form undoubtedly recommended it to the administrators of the Sailor Snug Harbor complex on Staten Island, New York. Captain's Cottage No. 2 (pp. 59-62) is one of several such residences built to house retired seamen. Despite its charming profile and decorative elements, there is nothing very fancy about the dwelling. The concave second-story roof is finished, as was customary, in a combination of fish-scale and fancy straight-cut shingles. The dormer windows, situated on all four sides of the building, feature "eye-brow" window caps. The upper roof is only slightly peaked, allowing little storage space; the first floor, however, is raised high enough above ground level to allow for effective use of the full basement. This lower level gains welcome natural light from windows positioned along the building's sides.

In keeping with its basic utilitarian purposes, the cottage has no grand staircase or center hall but, rather, a set of tightly-wound stairs in one corner. The first floor is a model of simplicity; its two large, airy rooms are equipped with fireplaces vented through a common central chimney. Behind these two spaces is a much smaller kitchen and pantry wing. The second floor is divided into three bedrooms, the largest separated by a central hallway extending from the stairs. The arrangement must have seemed more than adequate for men used to the close quarters of life at sea.

Captain Edward Penniman, whose home is illustrated on pp. 63-65, desired a more commodious residence. A whaling captain, he could enjoy a view of the Atlantic Ocean from the cupola atop this handsome building. Fancy capped chimneys are positioned at each side of the house. The first floor is divided by a wide center hall with parlors in the front sections and a kitchen and dining room behind them. Bay window alcoves extend from one of the parlors and the dining room. No doubt the home was kept absolutely ship-shape; built-in storage units are assets in every one of the rooms.

Four well-proportioned bedrooms and a bath are located on the second floor, each well lighted by dormer windows. A second set of stairs provides access to the rear bedrooms, the bath, and the third, or attic-floor, level. Plenty of space is found here for storage, and the attic receives light on all four sides from small triangular dormers.

Captain's Cottage No. 2, Sailors' Snug Harbor, New Brighton, Staten Island, New York, late 19th century, east elevation.

0   5'   15'

0   4
METERS 1:48

Cross section (north).

SECOND FLOOR
CEILING

9'-3"

SECOND FLOOR

11'-0 3/4"

29'-3 3/4"

FIRST FLOOR
WATER TABLE

9'-0"

BASEMENT
FLOOR

0   4
METERS

0   5'   15'

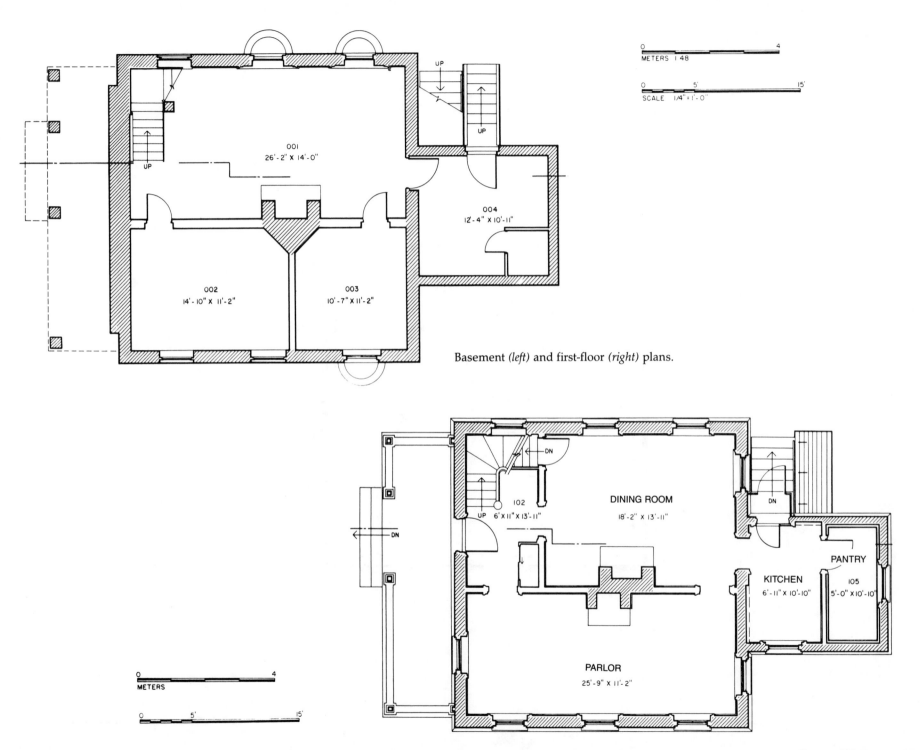

METERS 1 48

SCALE 1/4" = 1'-0"

001
26'-2" X 14'-0"

UP

UP

UP

004
12'-4" X 10'-11"

002
14'-10" X 11'-2"

003
10'-7" X 11'-2"

Basement *(left)* and first-floor *(right)* plans.

DN

102
6'X 11"X 13'-11"
UP

DN

DINING ROOM
18'-2" X 13'-11"

DN

PANTRY

KITCHEN
6'-11" X 10'-10"

105
5'-0" X 10'-10"

PARLOR
25'-9" X 11'-2"

METERS

Second-floor plan.

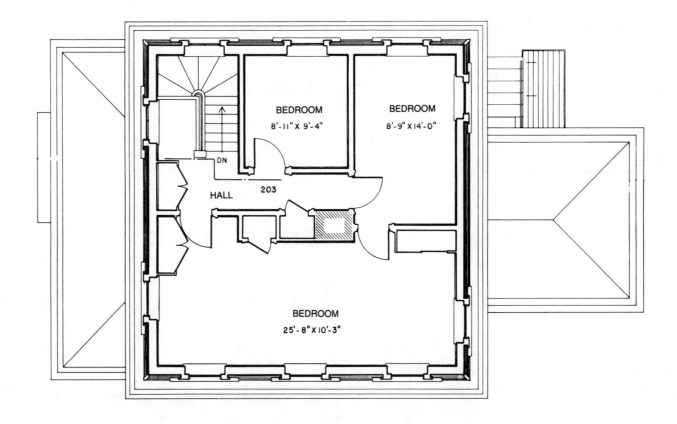

BEDROOM
8'-11" X 9'-4"

BEDROOM
8'-9" X 14'-0"

DN

HALL

203

BEDROOM
25'-8" X 10'-3"

0   4
METERS

0   5'   15'
SCALE

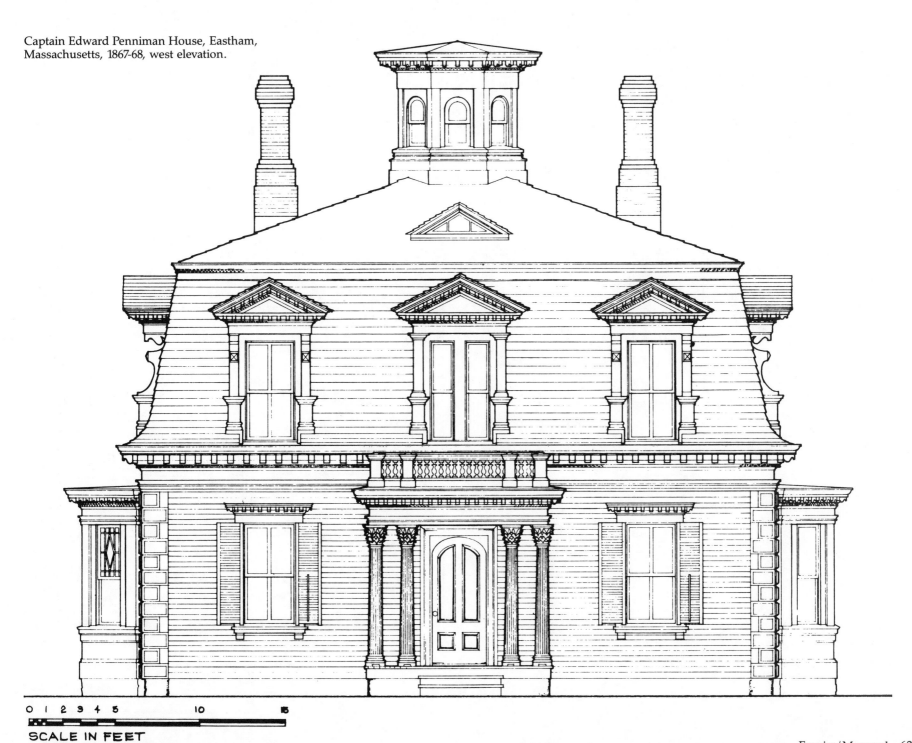

Captain Edward Penniman House, Eastham,
Massachusetts, 1867-68, west elevation.

0 1 2 3 4 5   10   15

SCALE IN FEET

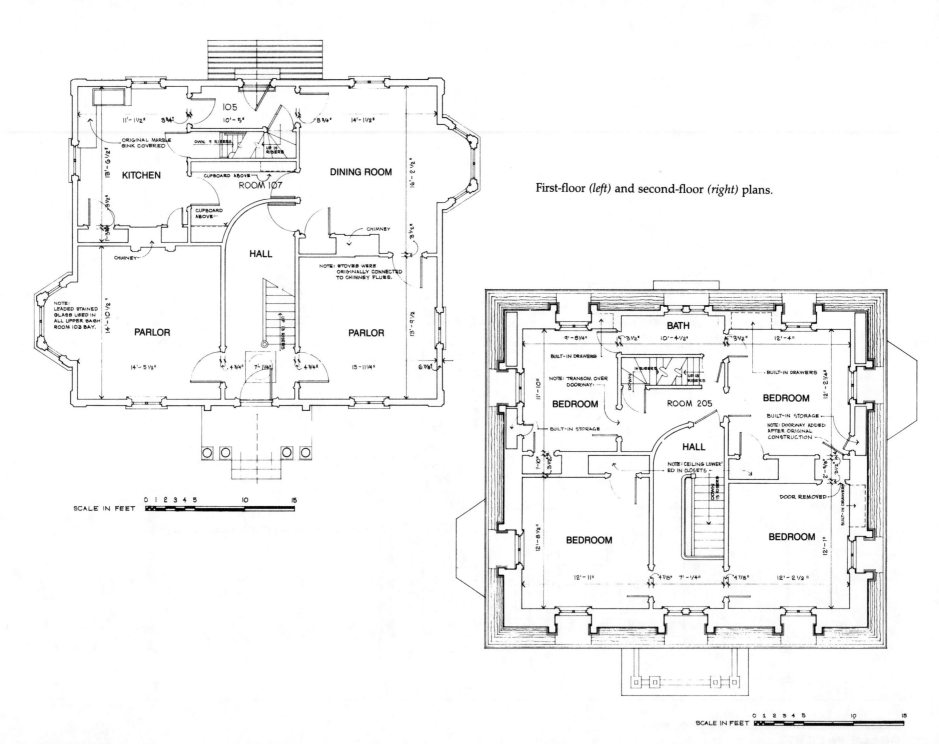

First-floor *(left)* and second-floor *(right)* plans.

First-floor plan (left)

105

11'-1½"   3¾"   10'-5"   8¾"   14'-1½"

ORIGINAL MARBLE
SINK COVERED   DWN. 9 RISERS   UP 14
RISERS

16'-2½"

KITCHEN   DINING ROOM

CUPBOARD ABOVE   ROOM 107

3½"

CUPBOARD
ABOVE   3½"

CHIMNEY

3½"

HALL   CHIMNEY   NOTE: STOVES WERE
ORIGINALLY CONNECTED
TO CHIMNEY FLUES.

CHIMNEY   6⅞"

NOTE:
LEADED STAINED   14'-10½"   13'-9½"
GLASS USED IN
ALL UPPER SASH   UP 13 RISERS
ROOM 103 BAY.

PARLOR   PARLOR

14'-5½"   4¾"   7'-1¼"   4¾"   13'-11¼"

SCALE IN FEET   0 1 2 3 4 5   10   15

Second-floor plan (right)

BATH

9'-8¼"   3½"   10'-4½"   3½"   12'-4"

BUILT-IN DRAWERS   14 RISERS   UP 13
RISERS   BUILT-IN DRAWERS

NOTE: TRANSOM OVER
DOORWAY.   DOWN   12'-2¼"

11'-10"   BEDROOM   ROOM 205   BEDROOM

BUILT-IN STORAGE

BUILT-IN STORAGE   NOTE: DOORWAY ADDED
AFTER ORIGINAL
CONSTRUCTION

1'-10"   3½"   HALL

NOTE: CEILING LOWER-
ED IN CLOSETS   2'-6½"   3½"

DOOR REMOVED

DOWN
13 RISERS   BUILT-IN DRAWERS

12'-8½"   BEDROOM   BEDROOM   12'-1"

12'-11"   4⅞"   7'-1¼"   4⅞"   12'-2½"

SCALE IN FEET   0 1 2 3 4 5   10   15

Sectional view.

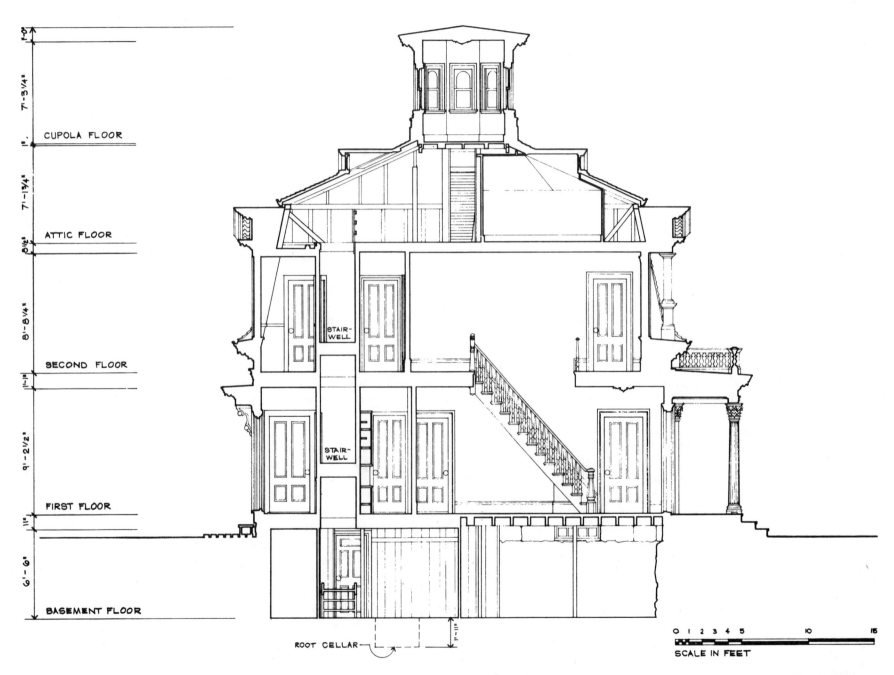

1'-0"

7'-3¼"

CUPOLA FLOOR

1"

7'-1¾"

ATTIC FLOOR

8½"

8'-8¼"

SECOND FLOOR

11"

9'-2½"

FIRST FLOOR

11"

6'-6"

BASEMENT FLOOR

STAIR-
WELL

STAIR-
WELL

ROOT CELLAR

1'-11"

0 1 2 3 4 5   10   15

SCALE IN FEET

With the exception of Colonial, the Queen Anne is the most readily recognizable style in North America, one practically synonymous with "Victorian." The multifaceted façades of such buildings are so striking that it is impossible to ignore them wherever they are found—in San Francisco, notably, or in Boston, or in Keokuk, Iowa. To define this style, however, is a more difficult exercise. "Queen Anne" is a term which, in the words of an 1883 critic, "has been made to cover a multitude of incongruities, including indeed, the bulk of recent work which otherwise defies classification, and there is a convenient vagueness about the term which fits it to that use." Ever since the Philadelphia Centennial Exposition of 1876, where half-timbered designs were executed by the British government, home builders and architects seized whatever elements of the style, launched by Richard Norman Shaw in England in 1868, struck their particular fancy. The earliest designs were inspired by Elizabethan forms, but these were gradually subsumed in a novel mixture of the Second Empire or Mansard, Shingle, and Stick styles.

The terminology of the 1880s is no less confusing. Contemporary books of house plans speak of Queen Anne, Elizabethan, and Eastlake styles. Modern day critics continue along the same vein, some substituting the jarring neologism "Jacobethan" for the Elizabethan and Jacobean, but retaining Queen Anne and Eastlake. Distinctions *can* be made between the three modes, and an attempt at doing so is tried here, but for all intents and purposes the term "Queen Anne" can be employed to cover a multitude of architectural virtues and sins. "Elizabethan" or "Jacobethan" refer to parapeted roofs, towers and turrets, and pseudo strapwork ornamentation. "Eastlake" refers to the lavish use of machine-turned architectural elements such as balusters and posts. These are seen most clearly on houses built in the San Francisco area during the 1880s and '90s. English architect Charles Eastlake, the author of *Hints on Household Taste* (first American edition, 1872), was astounded to discover in the 1880s that his designs for domestic furniture had been appropriated for architectural millwork. Many of the structural elements do give the appearance of being turned on a lathe in the same manner as tables and chair legs. In general form, however, "Eastlake" houses do not differ from the Queen Anne. In fact, a recent guide to building styles and terms, *Identifying American Architecture* by John J.-G. Blumenson, uses pictures of the same houses to identify both styles.

What then is a Queen Anne house? It is foremost a strongly asymmetrical building with steep gables, high chimneys, and a rich mixture of construction materials—wood, brick, and sometimes terra cotta, stone, and shingling. Attic and second-story gables often project well beyond lower floors. A tower or turret may be tucked into the side. Iron finials and cresting may appear at critical peaks. As in the Stick Style, porches and verandas sweep around several sides of the building.

The Short Hills, New Jersey, house (pp. 72-75) designed by the New York architectural firm of Lamb & Wheeler in the early 1880s displays many of the above features. The exterior walls are richly ornamented with terra-cotta panels and wood shingling of the fishscale variety, and lower surfaces are finished with wood clapboarding. The most distinctive element is the turreted oriel which appears almost to be hinged at the corner. The house features "triplet" windows in the parlor and in the oriel. Verandas and a porch extend around three sides of the dwelling. Chimneys are massive and capped in a decoratively flared fashion.

The interior decoration, as shown here, matches the exterior in style. The floor plans faithfully follow the cross-gabled form of the exterior. The first-floor rooms are generous spaces, the dining room being slightly larger than the parlor. The former is surely the most gracious room, with an opening to a back veranda and, presumably, landscaped grounds.

Beer baron Alfred Uihlein could well afford to build an imposing Queen Anne mansion (pp. 67-71). His palatial Milwaukee residence, however, occupied a surprisingly narrow lot. In consequence, the brick and stone building is almost as high as it is long; a corner tower climbs the full three stories and beyond. The interior spaces are as imposing and spacious as the grand exterior, with its massive brick chimneys and third-floor oriel window, would indicate. Maximum use is made of the tower space and two three-story bays to bring light and spatial interest to the principal rooms. Paneled wainscoting is utilized throughout the first-floor rooms and is used to dramatic effect to define the grand main staircase which opens off the front foyer.

The parlor of the Uihlein house is not merely a double, but a triple one, the front area serving as a reception room. It is here that the highly decorative fireplace (p. 69), with its Eastlake detailing, is found. The other connecting parlors serve as music room and library. Three principal second-story bedrooms are located near the front of the house, each laid out to include tower or bay window alcoves. Two other bedrooms, presumably for children, are at the back of the house, while servants' quarters are located on the third floor. Here, too, is a grand ballroom and cloak room where guests could leave their wraps.

John B. Lindale of Delaware was also a tycoon, but his wealth was in peaches rather than beer. His mansion (pp. 76-77) was thus situated on the farm. The veranda which tucks around the front and two sides of the frame structure is ideally suited for a rural setting. Like the Uihlein mansion, the basic form of the Lindale House is assymetrical. In this case, however, there are two three-story towers positioned on either side of the building, rather than the single tower of the Milwaukee house. Each of the Lindale House towers is covered with diamond and square-cut shingles, as is the main roof.

The principal first-floor rooms and second-floor bedrooms are irregularly-shaped areas which make imaginative use of the tower space and a two-story bay. The large two-over-two sash windows provide more than ample light and air. At the rear of the house is a raised one-story attached summer kitchen, an appropriate extension for a farmhouse, with old-fashioned six-over-six sash indicating that it probably survives from an earlier period.

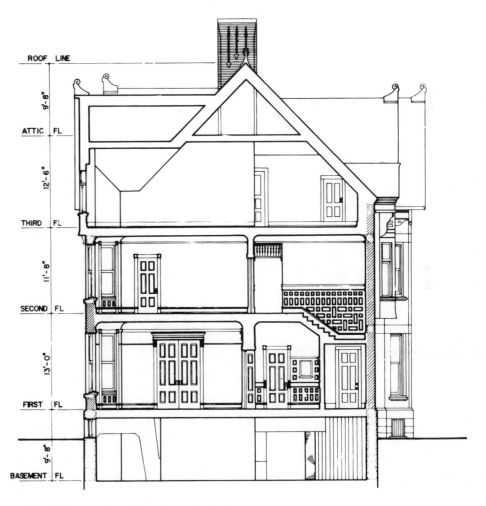

Alfred Uihlein House, Milwaukee, Wisconsin, 1887, Henry C. Koch and Co., architects, sectional view.

South elevation.

12'-6"

11'-8"

13'-0"

8'-8"

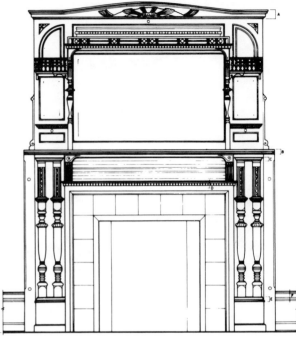

First-floor plan and front parlor fireplace elevation.

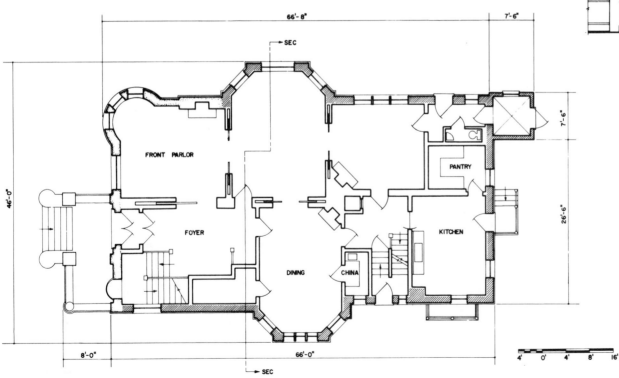

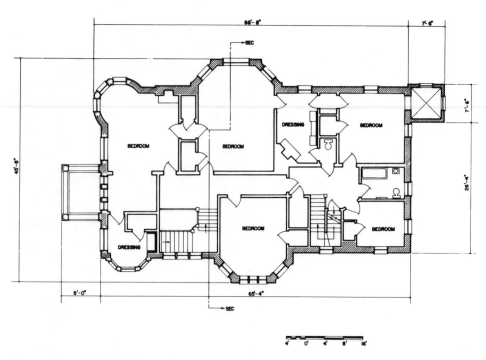

Second-floor and third-floor plans.

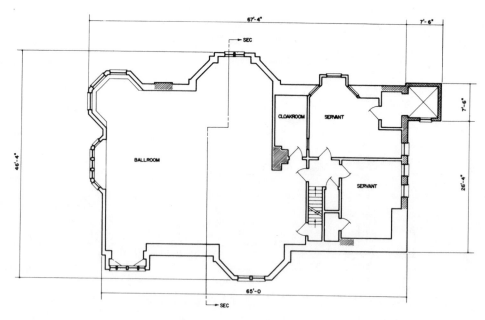

Typical interior door elevation, plan, and profiles.

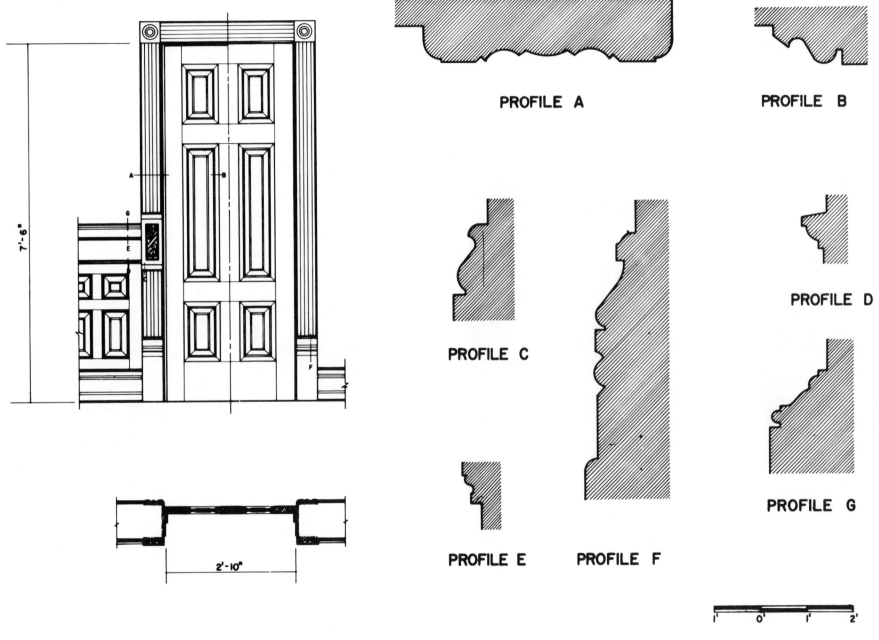

PROFILE A

PROFILE B

PROFILE C

PROFILE D

PROFILE E

PROFILE F

PROFILE G

7'-6"

2'-10"

1' 0' 1' 2'

Residence, Short Hills, New Jersey, 1881, Lamb
and Wheeler, architects, perspective view.

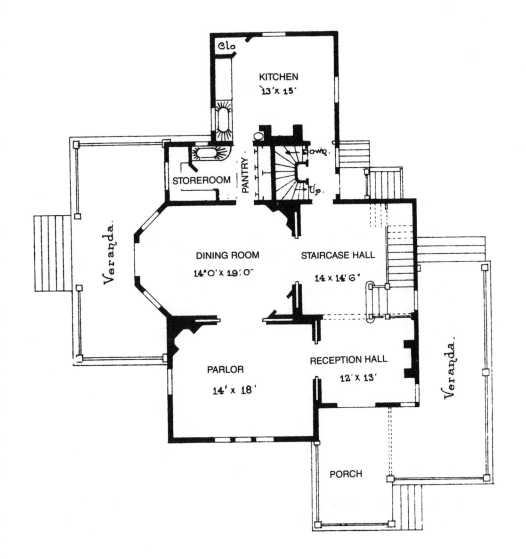

First-floor and second-floor plans.

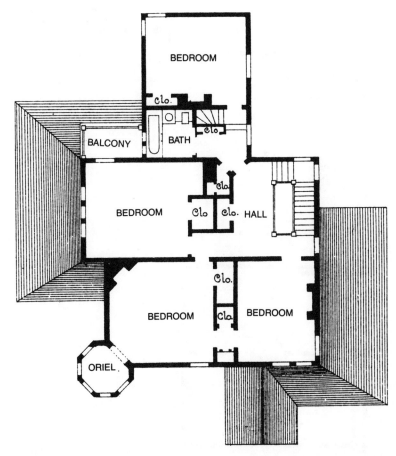

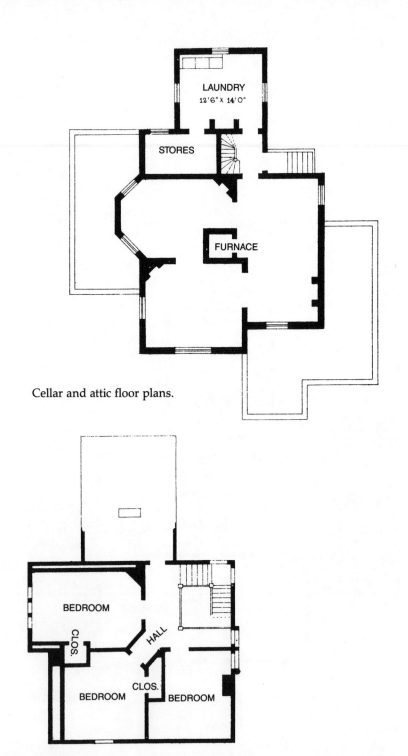

Cellar and attic floor plans.

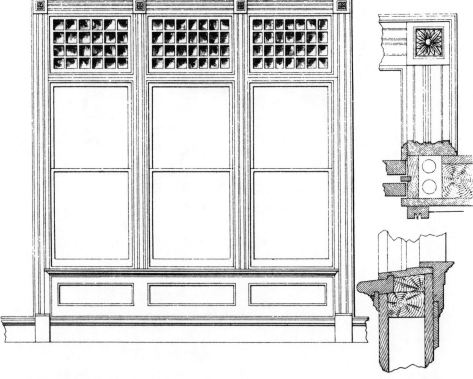

Triplet window and window section.

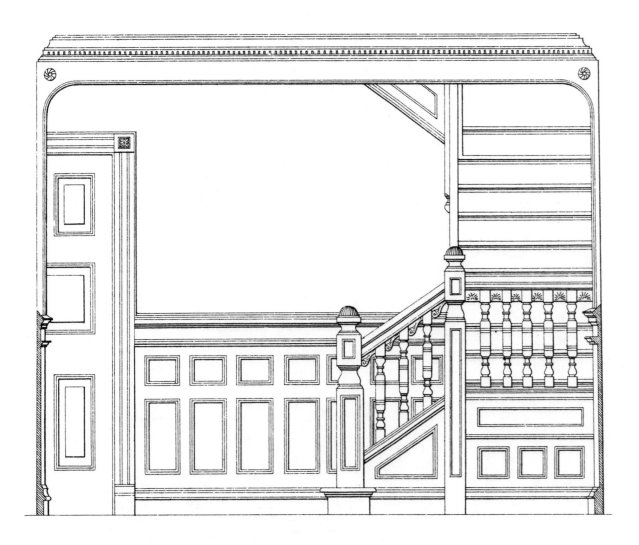

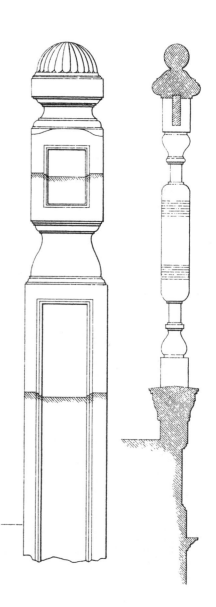

Hall interior, newel, and baluster rail.

John B. Lindale House, Magnolia, Delaware,
c. 1905, Charles G. Fisher, architect, south elevation.

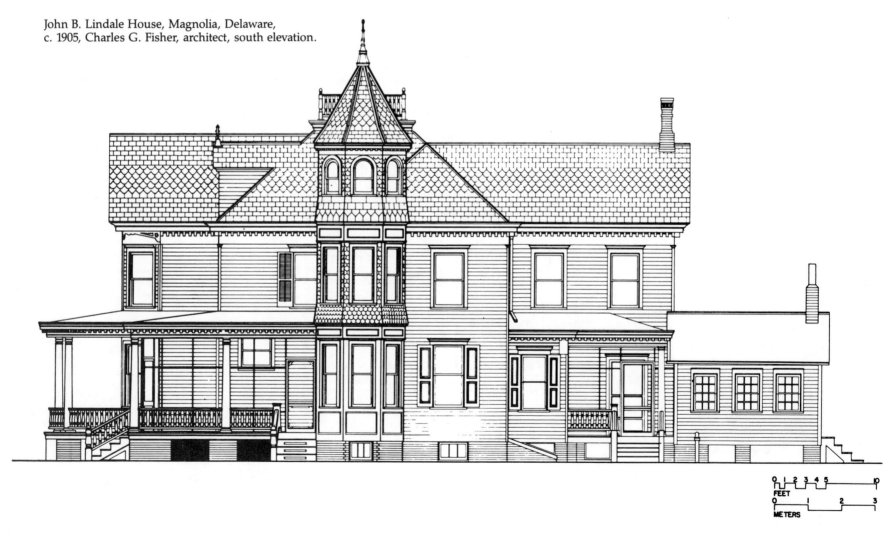

First-floor and second-floor plans.

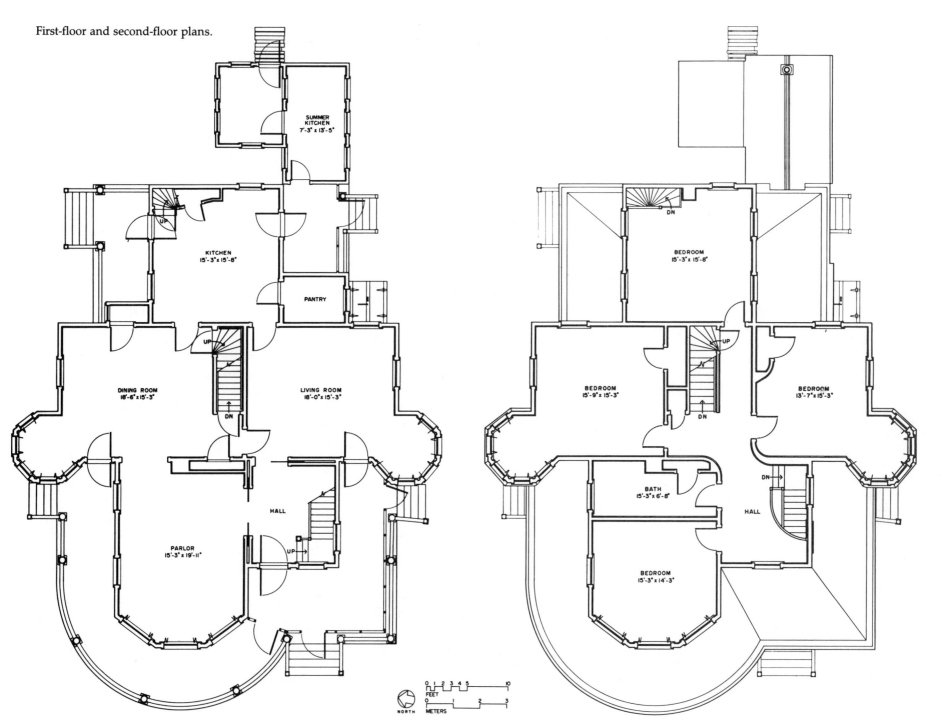

SUMMER
KITCHEN
7'-3" x 13'-5"

KITCHEN
15'-3" x 15'-8"

UP

PANTRY

DINING ROOM
18'-6" x 15'-3"

UP

DN

LIVING ROOM
18'-0" x 15'-3"

HALL

PARLOR
15'-3" x 19'-11"

UP

BEDROOM
15'-3" x 15'-8"

DN

UP

BEDROOM
15'-9" x 15'-3"

DN

BEDROOM
13'-7" x 15'-3"

BATH
15'-3" x 6'-8"

DN

HALL

BEDROOM
15'-3" x 14'-3"

0 1 2 3 4 5   10
FEET

0   1   2   3
METERS

NORTH

Well-to-do Americans of the late nineteenth century, increasingly successful in the affairs of the industrial marketplace, sought comfortable, fashionable dwelling places worthy of their new prosperity. Smaller homes closer to growing center cities were abandoned for green suburban estates. Truly successful men of business could afford to build yet a second new house, a vacation retreat for their families along an unspoiled coastal area or amidst mountain greenery. At first the new homes—suburban or vacation—were baronial in style, imitating the Stick Style or deriving from the Jacobean-style country houses popularized by Richard Norman Shaw and other British architects in the 1870s. By the 1880s, however, a more American form—the Shingle Style—was emerging.

As in so many matters of American architectural style, Henry Hobson Richardson was preeminent as a spokesman. The vertical thrust of the Stick Style and the Jacobean gave way in his plans to much greater horizontality. Wood paneling and half-timber construction were replaced on exterior surfaces with horizontal shingling. Certain elements of a seventeenth-century Colonial American style came into reuse—the gambrel roof; simple building materials such as wood shingles; a snug, close-to-the-earth profile. Americans had rediscovered their colonial heritage in the decade following the Centennial celebration, and while they still aped English manners, the leaders in style were receptive to the new architectural aesthetic. As numerous historians have explained, it was the beginning of a new era in building.

The elements of the style are unmistakable, and very much in evidence in the home built for H. K. Wilcox (pp. 82-83) in Middletown, New York, by a Richardsonian disciple, E. G. W. Dietrich. Here is found a blending of Colonial Revival and Romanesque forms as well as reminders of the past Gothic tradition. The broadly-shaped gambrel roof of the center portion of the house flows down and is anchored on a stone Romanesque base. This vast expanse of roof is broken with a fanlight and a row of shuttered, double-sash windows, and overhangs an arched entryway and a single bay window. On the side of the house, a massive chimney has been tucked into the sloping angle of the central gambrel; aside it is a second gambrel broken by a Palladian window, a double bay, and a single bay window. As if to pay proper respect to the Gothic Revival past, a lancet window appears in the front façade (in a room designated as the "library"). The bay windows and diamond-shaped panes in some of the sashes are further evidence of a lingering nostalgia for Gothic taste.

As eclectic as it is, the overall conception and composition of the Dietrich-designed house is Richardsonian and in the Shingle Style. The angles of the gambrels define the structure in every respect, sweeping down to include the side and back porches. Gambrels and porches, as Vincent Scully has written concerning the work of a similar architect, are interwoven "in a direct expression of continuity between interior and exterior spaces." The first and second floor plans testify to that basic plan.

From the massive Romanesque entryway one enters a vestibule and grand reception hall. This central space, with its monumental staircase as the focus, provides an entryway to all rooms of the house and largely determines their function. Prominently positioned on the front side of the house are the parlor, with working fireplace, and library with a massive hearth and bay window seats. Immediately behind these two areas are slightly less important rooms: a den with fireplace and, on the other side of the center hall, the dining room which opens up to the butler's pantry, and thus to the kitchen. A small conservatory is attached to a corner of the dining area. The architect has also allowed for movement between the dining area and the library, an agreeable arrangement for gentlemen wishing to retire from table to easy chair. Service areas of the house are properly positioned at the back of the house—butler's pantry, kitchen, cold storage area, pantry storage, and work room.

The second floor sleeping areas further testify to the elevated living style of the Wilcox family. The bedrooms are supplied with large storage closets and are well-lighted comfortable rooms, three of which are equipped with fireplaces. The master bedroom to the right is a particularly handsome area with a nook and window seats providing a private, cosy retreat. Again, as on the first floor, service rooms are positioned at the back—a servant's bedroom, and linen closets.

The firm of McKim, Mead and White, famous for its Beaux Arts mansions, deserves to be noted for homes in the Shingle Style as well. The Isaac Bell House (pp. 79-81) was designed by the firm as a summer cottage and is shingled throughout its rambling profile. The residence is typical of many built on the New England seacoast during the late 1800s for wealthy summer vacationers. As the east elevation shows, the building is overwhelmingly horizontal and assymetrical in composition; gables intersect gables and rounded projections play off a low wrap-around veranda. The roof line is punctuated by four massive chimneys; fireplaces on the first and second floors are prominent interior architectural features. In a home used only during the summer months, a central heating system was rarely utilized; the chill of the evening hours was effectively countered by a cozy hearth fire. The massive fireplace in the entrance hall (p. 81), with its side bench and elaborately paneled and tiled surround, is much more than a practical feature; it is also a stylistic reminder of the central importance of the hearth in the well-appointed home of the time. Not since the Colonial period had so much symbolic emphasis been given to the fireplace.

The floor plan of the three-story home is relatively open and makes maximum use of the imaginative outlines of the building. Some of these large, inviting spaces on the first floor have since been partitioned (indicated on plan by dotted lines), an unfortunate but probably necessary nod to twentieth-century convenience.

The Sheepshead Bay house (pp. 84-85) is a more modest and symmetrical design. Its overall shingling and the broad sweeping roof line which enfolds the wrap-around veranda distinguish it as a Shingle Style dwelling. This well-integrated design incorporates a three-story tower, a bay window, dormer windows, and two massive chimneys at the gable ends. The floor plan is quite straightforward, deviating from the straight line only to incorporate the tower and bay window. As in many later Prairie School houses, there is a seating alcove or inglenook tucked into the main stairwell recess.

Homes built in the Shingle Style made room for not only functional spaces but graceful, inviting areas—a conservatory for greenery; bay window nooks with built-in window seats for quiet moments; an open, center reception hall for the display of sculpture and other artwork; sweeping, curved porches for summer relaxation. This was a gilded age for those who could afford to enjoy it in high style.

Isaac Bell House, Newport, Rhode Island, 1882-83, McKim, Mead and White, architects, east elevation.

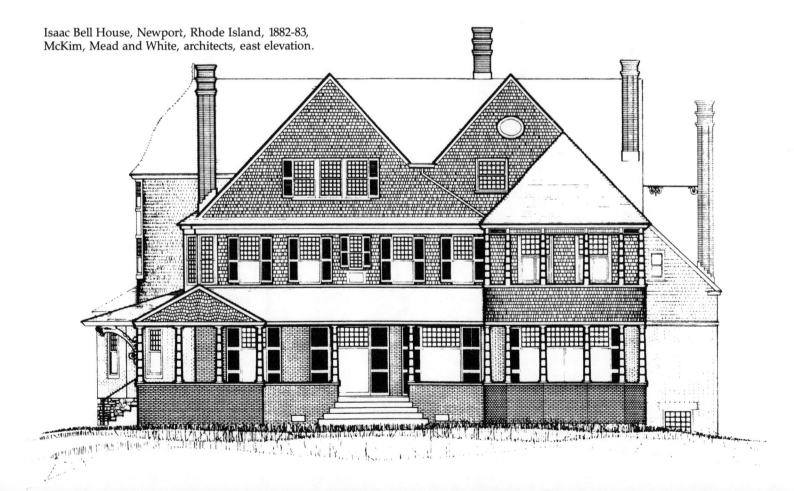

First-floor and second-floor plans.

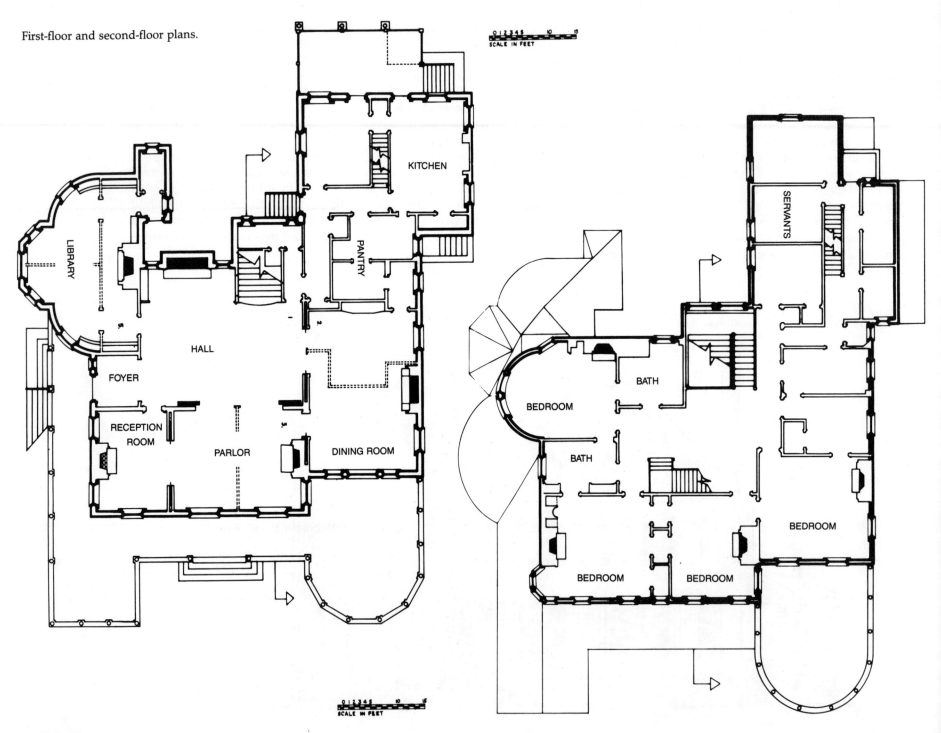

Hall fireplace, elevation.

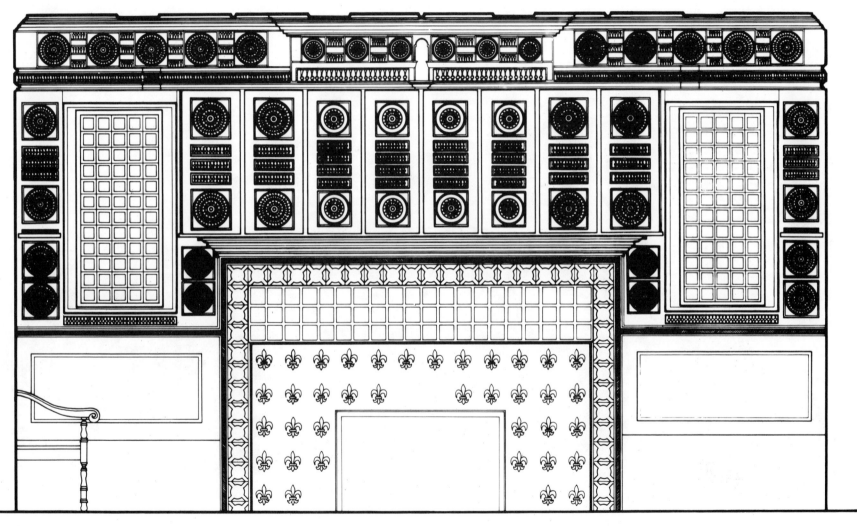

SCALE IN FEET

H. K. Wilcox Residence, Middletown, New York,
1891, E. G. W. Dietrich, architect, perspective.

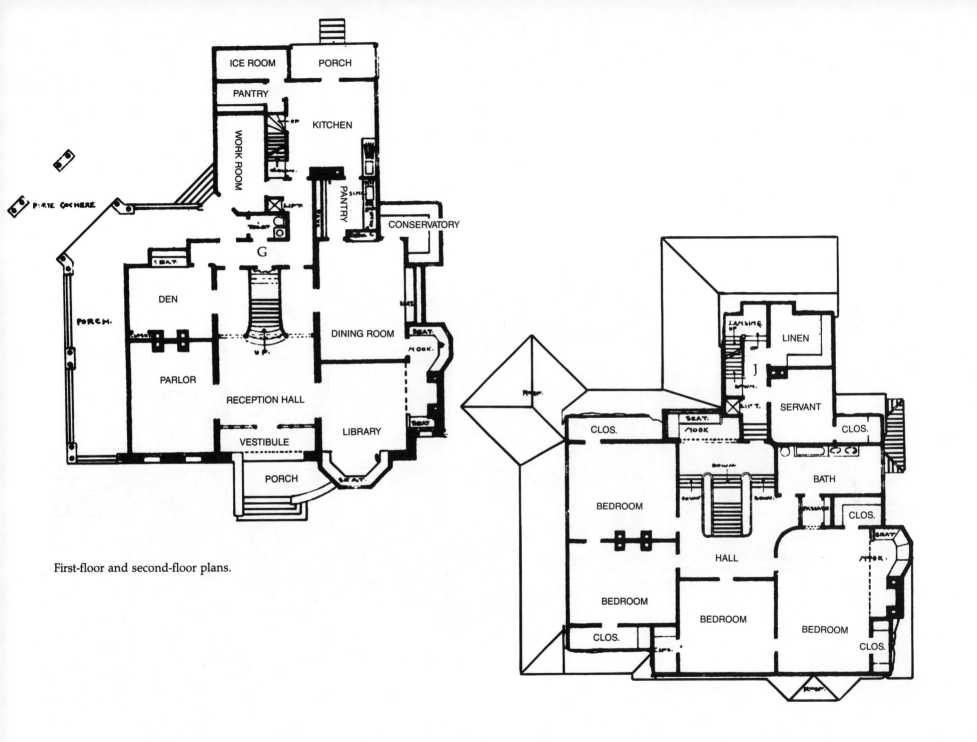

First-floor and second-floor plans.

Residence, Sheepshead Bay, Queens, New York, New York,
1897, Fowler and Hough, architects, perspective.

First-floor and second-floor plans.

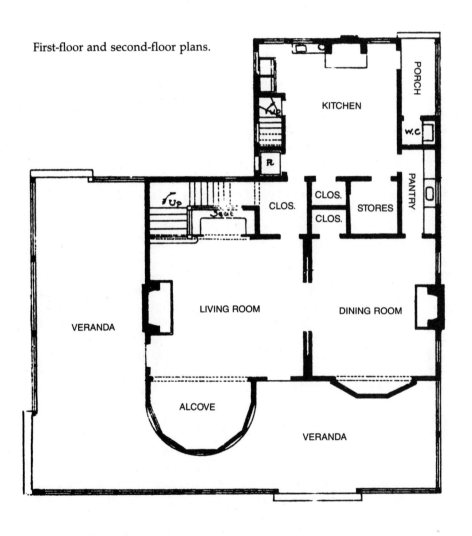

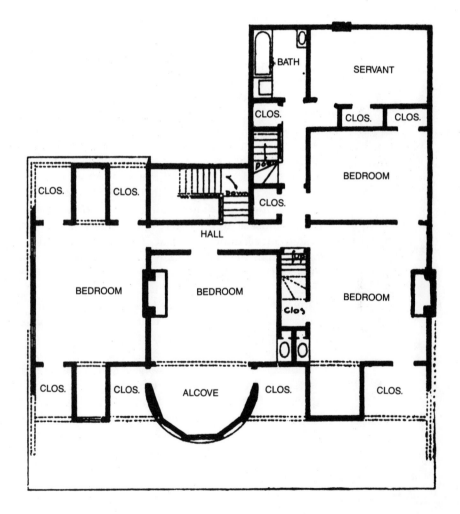

Romanesque forms are important component elements in the visual vocabulary of North American architecture. The semicircular arch was introduced during the 1840s in entrances and windows and persisted in use throughout the century under various stylistic guises—Romanesque Revival, Victorian Romanesque, and Richardsonian Romanesque. In addition to the arch, many brick and/or stone buildings featured such structural forms as the rounded buttress, curvilinear wall, and tower. The overall profile was often massive and was suited perfectly to such structures as churches, governmental offices, schools, and railroad stations. The Romanesque did not become a popular style for home building until the 1880s and '90s. Its great master and popularizer, Henry Hobson Richardson, died in 1886, and in his wake the architectural community strove to introduce the style in every possible way.

Many of the earliest buildings and all those of Richardson himself are relatively restrained in decoration and present a monochromatic masonry façade. Richardson's structures are unique in their utter dependence on mass and scale for their impact. The Glessner House in Chicago (1885), one of the masterpieces of American domestic architecture, depends for its character only on the placement of quarry-faced stone blocks and their relation to entryway arches, window openings, and a low roof line. Through the massing of shapes in an almost sculptured fashion, something truly original was created out of stone. The firm of Burnham and Root was equally successful in its interpretations of the Romanesque in such structures as The Rookery (1886) and the Ayer House (1885), both in Chicago.

The Romanesque, as applied to domestic architecture, was usually treated in a more ornamental manner, and such homes constitute by far a majority of buildings in this style. Exterior masonry walls were frequently rendered more decorative through the use of various colored and textured stone in bands, trim, and arches. This created a polychromatic effect which was picturesque, yet in keeping with a fortress-like appearance. Brick and terra-cotta tiles or panels were also used to emphasize and embellish structural elements such as windows, roof lines, gables, and entryways. This was the *Victorian* Romanesque, a vernacular style that balanced the ornamental with the functional, the vertical thrust of Gothic with the horizontal emphasis of the arch.

Such a fine balance is reflected in the Ira Heath residence (pp. 87-88), attributed to the firm of Adler & Sullivan. Quarried brownstone blocks form the exterior walls and a brick and stone belt course defines the first floor from the second. Stone has been employed for the door and window heads. Centered on the Gothic gable at the third-floor level is a decorative stone and brick half circle, a form which repeats the architectural treatment of the main entryway.

The Heath House is raised on a half basement, a common feature in such an urban row house. Deliveries and pickups would have been made through the lower entrance to the left. Unlike many Federal town houses of the early nineteenth century, however, the kitchen is not located in the basement, but on the first floor. Typical of the mid- to late-nineteenth century town house are the positioning of the main entrance at one side and the regular three-bay façade. While many noteworthy Romanesque buildings such as the Glessner House and Adler and Sullivan's great Auditorium Building in Chicago have blockish, horizontal profiles, the majority are as tall as they are deep or wide.

The Heath residence extends back into the lot in two sections, the first containing the "public" rooms and the second the dining and service areas. A spacious entry hall has been provided in the center, allowing for direct passage to both front and rear rooms. The monotonous floor plan of so many city dwellings built on narrow sites, with one room linked to another in "railroad flat" fashion, has thus been avoided.

Almost every kind of building material is employed in the Elizabeth Plankinton mansion (pp. 89-91), one of the glories of late-nineteenth-century Milwaukee. The principal medium is limestone, imaginatively used to define segmental arches, window and door openings, and the towering chimneys. Brick, terra cotta, and stucco further embellish and outline the multi-faceted façade. This is an urban castle; in place of an attached gatehouse there is a porte cochère where visitors could alight from their carriages.

In many respects, the building resembles the Queen Anne Uihlein House (pp. 67-71), also located in Milwaukee, but the repetition of the wedge-shaped Roman arch at every level defines the structure as being Romanesque. The interior details, however, follow those found in many other late-nineteenth-century mansions, Romanesque or not. Fireplaces are located in all of the principal rooms; elaborate wainscoting accents the walls of the entry hall, main stairway, and other first-floor spaces. Like the Uihlein mansion, the irregular floor plan contains numerous picturesque nooks and crannies. On the third floor there is a spacious ballroom.

Romanesque Style buildings of this sort have been a favorite target of the wrecker's ball in recent years, the Plankinton mansion being one of the victims. Their very monumentality seems to challenge destruction. Such stone- or brickwork buildings, of course, cannot be cosmetically treated quite as easily with paint as can frame structures. And given the quality of today's air, it is remarkable that the stonework of many such urban buildings has resisted severe corrosion. Consequently, such homes often present a bedraggled, down-at-the-heels appearance. Romanesque buildings have another strike against them—they often appear cold and forbidding to the modern eye. Although a few may be frightful mammoths best buried with the other bones of the past, the majority are surely much more imaginative and inviting domestic dwelling places than their modern jerry-built counterparts.

SCALE

Ira A. Heath House, Chicago, Illinois, c. 1889, attributed to Adler and Sullivan, architects, east elevation.

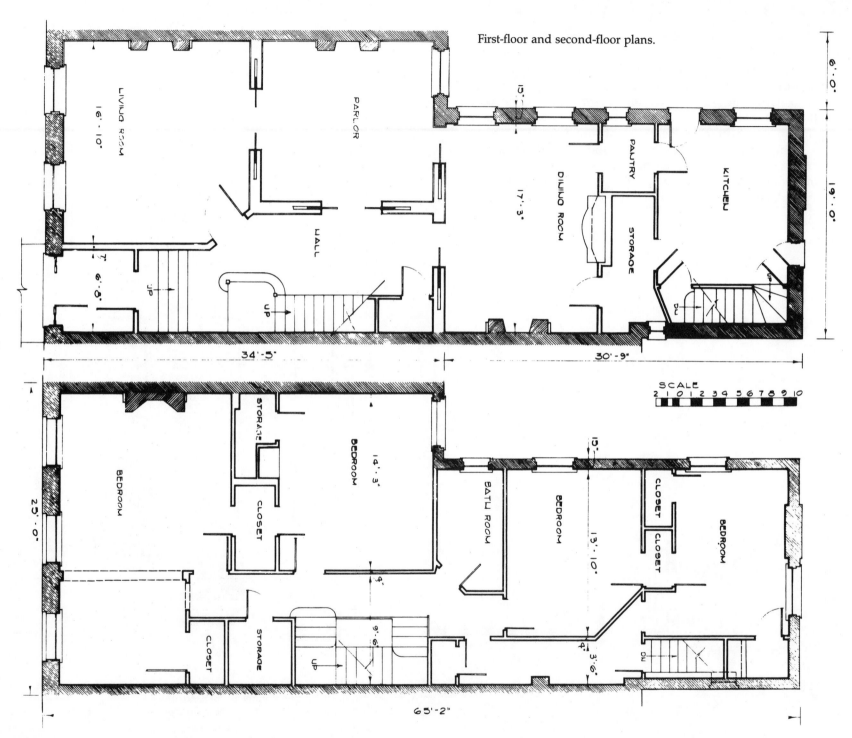

First-floor and second-floor plans.

LIVING ROOM
16'·10"

PARLOR

HALL

DINING ROOM
17'·3"

PANTRY

STORAGE

KITCHEN

UP

UP

UP

DN

7'·?"

6'·8"

15'

6'·0"

19'·0"

34'·5"

30'·9"

SCALE
2 1 0 1 2 3 4 5 6 7 8 9 10

BEDROOM

STORAGE

CLOSET

BEDROOM
14'·3"

BATH ROOM

BEDROOM

CLOSET

CLOSET

BEDROOM

CLOSET

STORAGE

UP

DN

25'·0"

9"

9'·6"

13'·10"

15'

4'

3'·6"

65'·2"

Elizabeth Plankinton House, Milwaukee, Wisconsin, 1886-88,
Edward Townsend Mix, architect, south elevation.

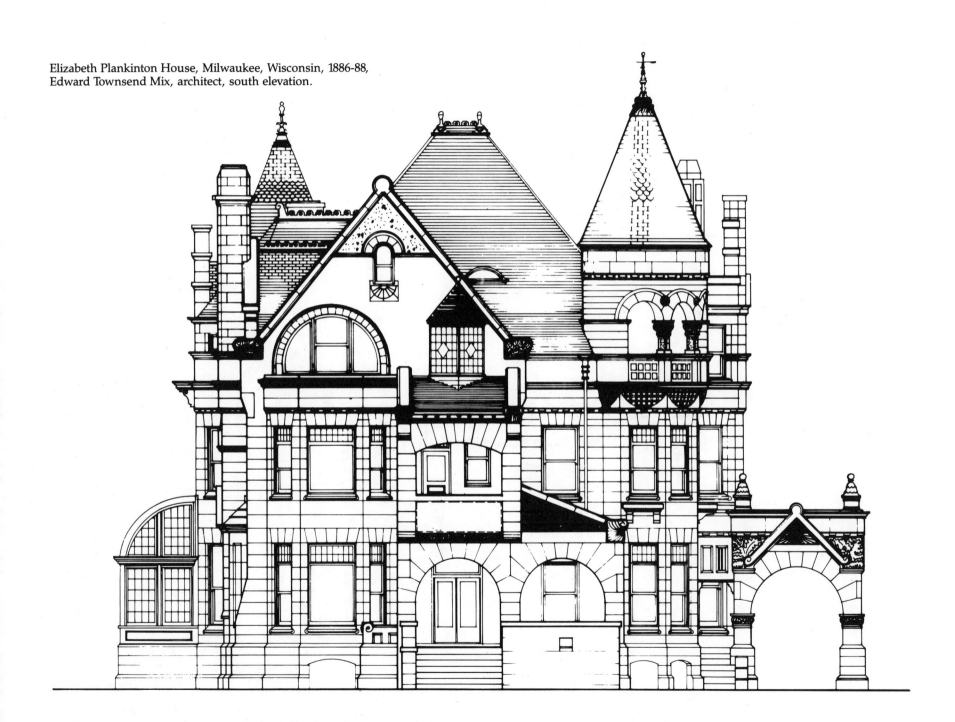

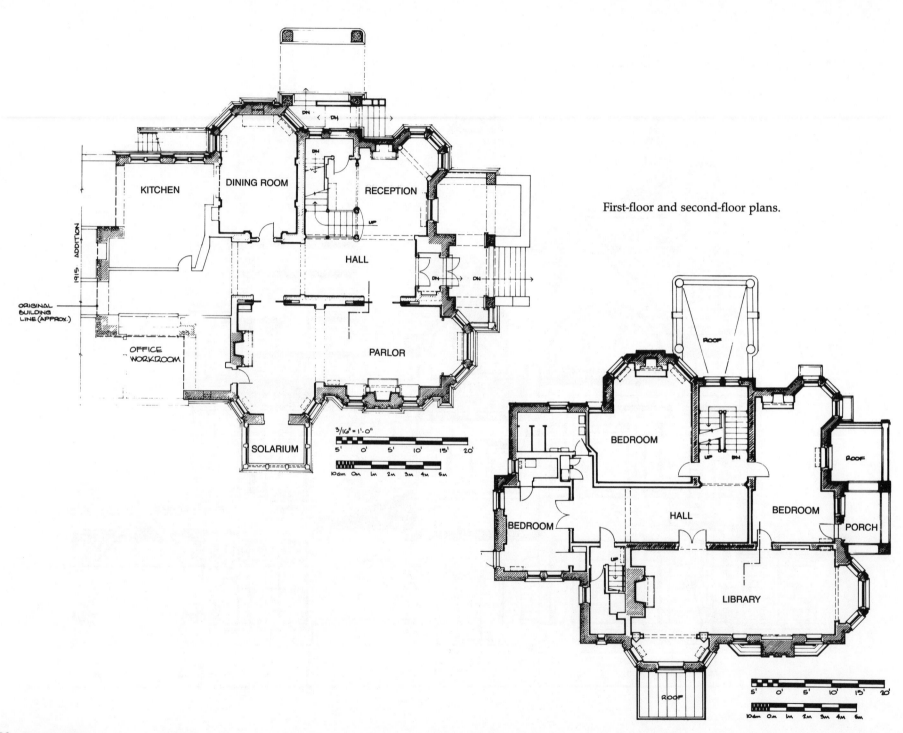

KITCHEN

DINING ROOM

RECEPTION

1915 ADDITION

ORIGINAL
BUILDING
LINE (APPROX.)

OFFICE
WORKROOM

HALL

PARLOR

SOLARIUM

DN

DN

DN

UP

DN

DN

3/16" = 1'-0"

5'   0'   5'   10'   15'   20'

10dm 0m   1m   2m   3m   4m   5m

First-floor and second-floor plans.

BEDROOM

ROOF

BEDROOM

HALL

BEDROOM

PORCH

ROOF

LIBRARY

ROOF

UP   DN

UP

5'   0'   5'   10'   15'   20'

10dm 0m   1m   2m   3m   4m   5m

Third-floor plan.

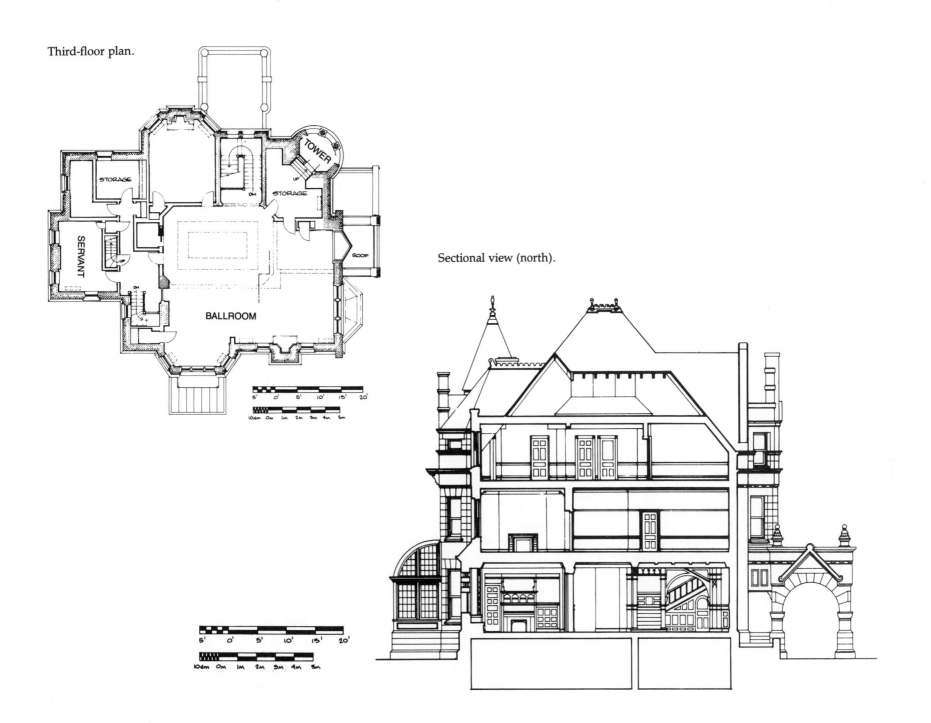

Sectional view (north).

STORAGE

TOWER

STORAGE

SERVANT

UP

DN

ROOF

BALLROOM

UP

DN

5' 0' 5' 10' 15' 20'

10dm 0m 1m 2m 3m 4m 5m

5' 0' 5' 10' 15' 20'

10dm 0m 1m 2m 3m 4m 5m

Nostalgia for the 1920s, the last period before the trauma of Depression, is widely expressed and indulged today. The building styles of the period, however, are just being reexamined. In terms of architecture, the time was a "snobbish" one, and the English style has been rightly termed "Stockbroker's Tudor" by one critic. In a vainglorious search for proper antecedents, wealthy Americans of British descent not only sought to establish genealogical links with their Colonial and Waspish past, but aped the manners and copied the manor house style of days gone by. Entire English manor houses were brought to America and reconstructed with infinite care and expense. Various kinds of architectural ornamentation and structural elements, of course, were ripped away from their European roots with the signing of sufficiently large checks. The Gatsbys of the time, although unable to establish a right to join the Sons of the American Revolution or the Order of St. George, fell right in with the antiquarian spirit.

Wealthy Americans turned to several building forms for their dream houses. The massive, half-timbered manor of the Jacobean sort, with gate house, stable, and other dependencies, was one suitable prototype. Architect Richard Norman Shaw had interpreted this form in the English countryside and in London's Bedford Park neighborhood during the 1860s and '70s, and Henry Hobson Richardson followed in somewhat the same direction for a period of time in America with considerable originality. Richardson moved on to articulate the Shingle Style; lesser talents interpreted the English heritage in more conventional ways. The style was known as "Elizabethan" at the time, and was, in fact, a variant of the Queen Anne. By the 1920s, what had been called "Elizabethan" had disappeared from view along with the Queen Anne style of building. The new English Tudor was a more "correct" form in that it imitated an historical style with greater fidelity. Fortunately, however, the best architects at work in the Tudor genre were not slavish to the past, and few devoted their time exclusively to sprawling country estates.

More modest in size than the manor house was the stone Cotswold cottage. Considerably larger than the term suggests to Americans, it was, nonethless, scaled down not only in size but in the extent of its ornamentation. Suburban areas of Philadelphia, especially the Chestnut Hill section, are composed of homes directly inspired by the humbler tradition of Cotswold masonry construction. Harold Donaldson Eberlein, an estimable critic and historian of American architecture in the early decades of this century, thought the Cotswold form an ideal one for suburban houses, and

argued that, "To revert to the Cotswold type of architecture for present inspiration in domestic design . . . is neither . . . a bit of affectation and archaeological pedantry, nor a piece of Anglo maniac inanity. It is only asserting our indefeasible right to a lawful part of our national heritage." Eberlein was, of course, projecting his own social prejudices and those of the class he served. Nevertheless, a close look at the stone homes of Chestnut Hill that he was defending leads one to the conclusion that he was right—for whatever reason. Again, in his own words, "No attempt was made to *reproduce* any Cotswold house, or group of houses; that would have been foolish. But by drawing inspiration from Cotswold models for the general manner of treatment and by making such adaptations as the needs of the individual case dictated, a result was achieved wholly satisfactory to all concerned—including the occupants, harmonious with the natural environment, and consistent in the employment of materials native to the locality. What more could any one desire?"

Now that English Tudor is taking its place along with the Colonial Revival in the pantheon of officially recognized historical styles, there is little reason for questioning its *raison d'etre*. What remains is the detailed examination of the elements which define the style and provide a means for its evaluation. This is no simple matter. "English" Tudor houses are decidedly North American—just as the Georgian Colonial and Italianate were naturalized—and combine in varying degrees elements of Norman, Elizabethan, and Jacobean styles. Some houses are overwhelmingly severe or Romanesque in profile, and others display the full richness of the late Tudor style—strapwork, parapets, projecting bays. The most commonly encountered exterior feature is that of half-timbering. This is seen in almost all of the nineteenth-century houses illustrated on the following pages and is a common motif on many English Tudor homes of the twentieth century. The timbering assumes the forms of both strapwork ornamentation in the gables and of vertical panels below, these exposed structural bands alternating with stuccoing or plasterwork.

Varied aspects of the style in America can be seen in the "Elizabethan" design of 1881 (p. 99), the heavily-shingled Double House of 1887 (pp. 94-95), Bertram Goodhue's 1891 imitation of a Norman Shaw English suburban house (p. 91), and the Tudor mansion of the Scaife family built c. 1920 (pp. 96-98). It is the most recent house of these four which is most fully "Tudor" in spirit and least "Elizabethan." There is no timbering of any sort but, rather, a massing of Perpendicular Gothic forms such as the four-centered pointed arches of the windows and doors. The style expressed in the Scaife mansion is more commonly encountered on a college campus, where it is better known as Collegiate Gothic.

Most English Tudor homes are of frame or brick construction or a combination of both. The style is highly picturesque and for this reason is being revived today in suburban developments. Unfortunately, the ornamental elements of these new houses often lack depth and character; they appear to be gratuitous. The timbering of most early twentieth-century homes appears real—not simulated. More ambitious home owners carried period detailing even further with the addition of such features as carved stone ornaments, cast terra-cotta forms, and casement windows.

Every metropolitan area in North America contains its neighborhood of older English Tudor homes—large and small.

Some of these feature eaves sweeping almost to the ground, providing an arched shelter for an entryway or garage. This particular form suggests the influence of Richardson and his followers in the early Queen Anne and in the Shingle styles. The overall perspective is one of overwhelming horizontality, a tying of the structure to its site. This appreciation of the natural environment is also expressed by the use of fine building materials in grand and modest homes—good hardwoods, fieldstone, terra cotta, copper and zinc, leaded glass, cast and wrought iron. The craftsmanship and quality of materials displayed in many such homes now located in declining neighborhoods make them especially attractive real estate investments. Only their spacious dimensions pose problems for the energy-conscious owner.

Residence, 1891, Bertram Goodhue, architect, perspective.

Double house design, late 19th century, from *Palliser's New Cottage Homes* (1887), front and end perspectives.

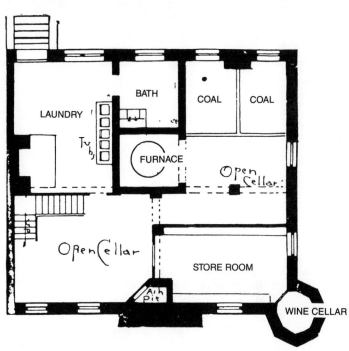

Half-cellar plan.

LAUNDRY BATH COAL COAL

Tubs FURNACE Open Cellar

Open Cellar STORE ROOM

Ash Pit WINE CELLAR

First-floor plan.

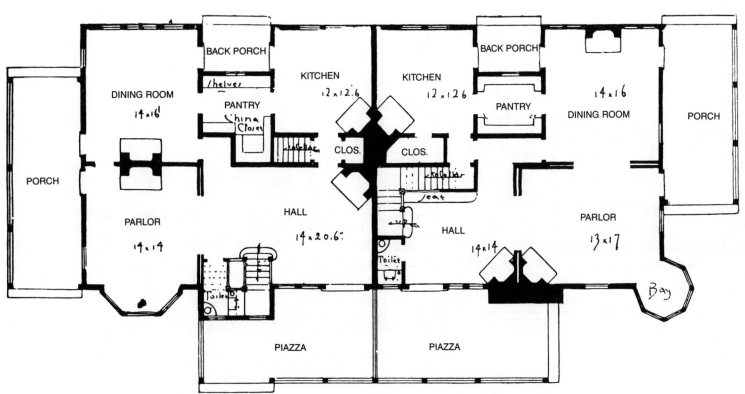

PORCH

DINING ROOM 14 x 16'

Shelves

BACK PORCH

PANTRY China Closet

KITCHEN 12 x 12.6

KITCHEN 12 x 12.6

BACK PORCH

PANTRY

DINING ROOM 14 x 16

PORCH

PARLOR 14 x 14

CLOS.

CLOS.

14 x 14

HALL 14 x 20.6"

cellar

seat

PARLOR 13 x 17

HALL 14 x 14

Toilet

Bay

Toilet

PIAZZA

PIAZZA

Alan M. Scaife Residence, Laughlintown vicinity,
Pennsylvania, early 20th century, west elevation.

SCALE

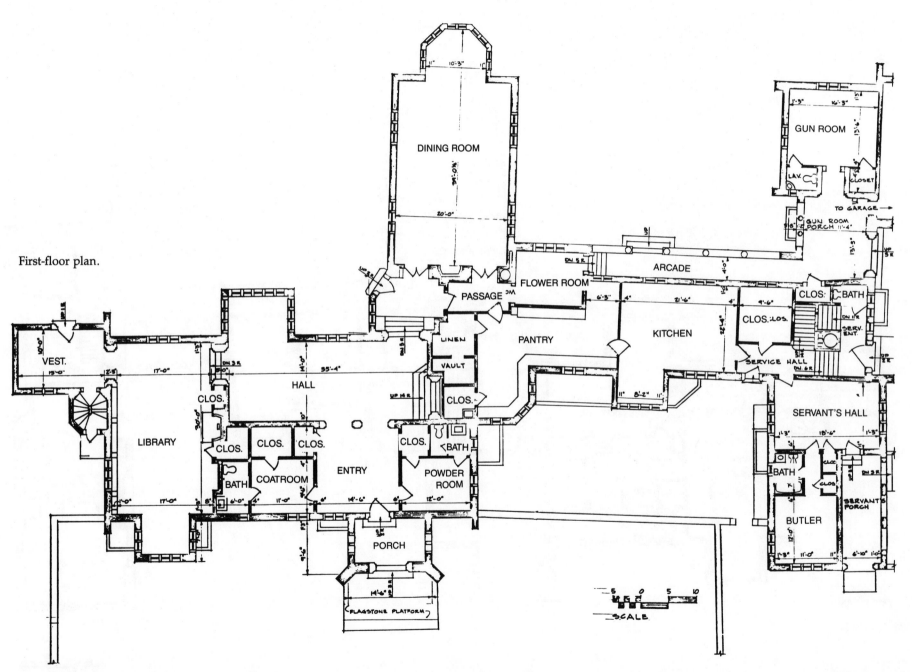

First-floor plan.

DINING ROOM

10'-3"

20'-0"

GUN ROOM

16'-3"

LAV.

CLOSET

TO GARAGE →

GUN ROOM PORCH 11'-4"

ARCADE

FLOWER ROOM

PASSAGE

KITCHEN

CLOS. BATH

CLOS.

CLOS.

SERV. ENT.

VEST.

15'-0"

17'-0"

35'-4"

HALL

LINEN

VAULT

PANTRY

6'-3"

21'-6"

4'-6"

SERVICE HALL

CLOS.

CLOS.

CLOS.

SERVANT'S HALL

LIBRARY

CLOS.

CLOS.

CLOS.

CLOS.

BATH

8'-2"

18'-6"

BATH

CLO.

BATH

COATROOM

ENTRY

POWDER ROOM

BUTLER

SERVANT'S PORCH

17'-0"

6'-0"

11'-0"

14'-6"

12'-0"

12'-0"

11'-0"

6'-10"

PORCH

14'-6"

FLAGSTONE PLATFORM

5 0   5   10

SCALE

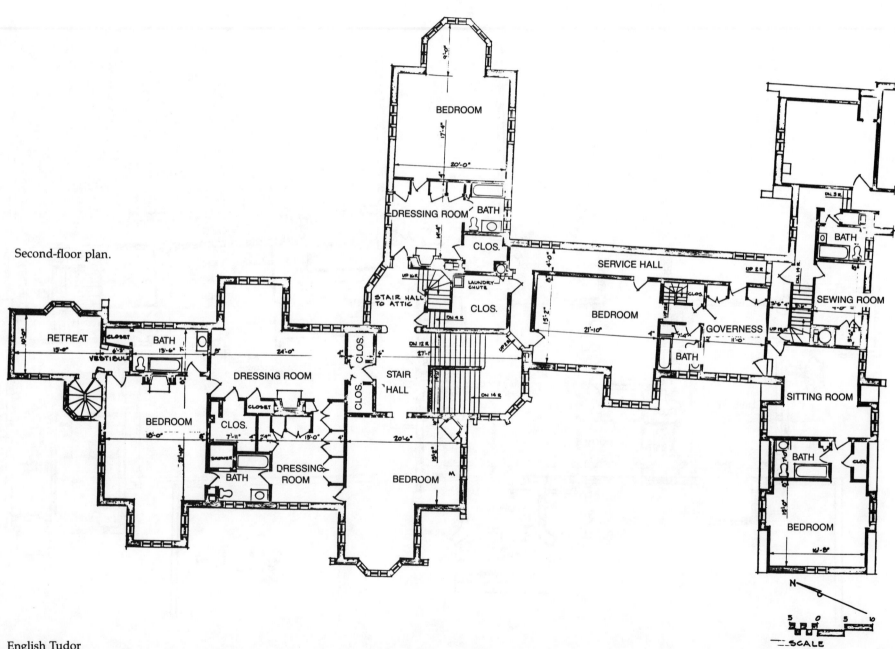

Second-floor plan.

BEDROOM

17'-4"
20'-0"

DRESSING ROOM   BATH

CLOS.

STAIR HALL
TO ATTIC

UP 16 R   LAUNDRY
CHUTE

CLOS.   CLOS.

SERVICE HALL   UP 2 R

BATH

SEWING ROOM

RETREAT

CLOSET   BATH

VESTIBULE   DRESSING ROOM

BEDROOM   21'-10"

GOVERNESS   UP 18 R

10'-0"   15'-0"   6'-3"   13'-6"   8"   24'-0"   4"   CLOS.   CLOS.   DN 12 R   UP 2 R   15'-2"   4'-0"   11'-0"

BEDROOM   CLOS.   CLOSET   CLOS.   STAIR HALL   DN 14 R   BATH   SITTING ROOM

18'-0"   7'-11"   7'-4"   13'-0"   4"   20'-6"

SHOWER   BATH   DRESSING ROOM   BEDROOM   M   BATH   CLOS.

15'-0"

BEDROOM

W-8"

N

5   0   5   0
SCALE

98   English Tudor

Elizabethan-style dwelling, 1881, from *Architectural Designs and Details*, elevations.

The Bungalow Style has recently been recognized as an important and imaginative American building form. For anyone schooled in the tradition that only Colonial or early nineteenth-century styles are worthy of study, a reference to something as undignified as a bungalow must come as somewhat of a shock. Architectural historians have occasionally sought to elevate the style with the use of the term "bungaloid," an unfortunate choice of words which only suggests a building rather lacking in attractive qualities. Bungalow is the term which has been used since the late 1800s—and so it shall remain.

Where does the word come from? It is thought to have been derived from the Hindu word *baṅglā*—a low, one-story building with a wide veranda—and may have entered the English vocabulary via the Anglo-Indian community in the nineteenth century. Bungalows were known in America by the 1880s; by the end of the century, the term was usually associated with a one-and-a-half-story California-style residence with a sloping gable roof that swept down over a front veranda. Dormer windows often protruded from the roof at the front and back of the house, thereby allowing the low upper story to be used for at least one bedroom and/or storage space.

The usual bungalow is a modest structure built on a fairly narrow lot and makes up in depth what it lacks in height. One or two bedrooms are usualy situated on the first floor behind a living room and dining area. This is the arrangement found in the Greenhouse Manager's House on Longview Farm (pp. 101-102). Many thousands of these dwellings were built throughout North America during the first several decades of the twentieth century. They were especially popular in the working-class neighborhoods of large cities in the Far West, the South, and the South Central states, as well as in rural areas. The bungalow, often termed a "California house," was an affordable alternative for most people; plans were published in all the popular building magazines which circulated throughout the country. Plans of developments similar to the Hanchett Residence Park in San Diego (p. 103) were widely distributed. The large mail-order companies could even ship you a prefabricated bungalow. The precursor of the ubiquitous ranch-style house—also born in California—the bungalow inspired romantic songs; it was the early 1900s equivalent of the pioneer log cabin.

Bungalows were built of wood, brick, or concrete blocks. Some were clapboarded, others stuccoed or shingled. The roof was usually shingled, but in the West and South might be formed of terra cotta tiles. Rafters and other structural members supporting the roof were sometime exposed along the overhang, giving the structure a rustic, hand-crafted appearance similar to that displayed in Gustav Stickley's Craftsman homes of the same period.

The bungalow, like the first ranch-style houses of the twentieth century, was originally intended for both outdoor and indoor living. The open veranda is usually supported at each end by two tapering columns or piers and a low balustrade or rail encloses the sides and front. Now it is not uncommon to find that the porch has been enclosed, either to gain living space or because it is no longer pleasant or safe to watch the passing neighborhood scene.

The fanciest of bungalows are those built around the turn of the century in California and designed by firms such as Greene and Greene. The Irwin House (pp. 104-107) is one of their most praised accomplishments. There is little resemblance between the common bungalow and this complex structure, which is built around a center courtyard. The Greene brothers' design is more clearly derived from Japanese sources than it is from the Anglo-Indian summer house. The Irwin House, nevertheless, can be viewed as an assemblage of two-story bungalows, each one of which is sheltered under a low-pitched overhanging roof. The term bungalow, like that of cottage a hundred years earlier, embraced a wide variety of buildings. In the early 1900s a hunting lodge was sometimes called a bungalow, as was many a seaside cottage.

The floor plan of the Irwin House shows just how imaginatively space can be used and how the structure can be integrated with the outdoors. In common with the humbler average bungalow, there is accommodation on the first floor for bedrooms, although in this case the principal bedrooms are located on the second floor. The interior appointments are similar to those found in any high style Mission or art and crafts period home—paneled shoulder-high wainscoting, massive fireplaces, window seats—all executed in natural materials and with a sensitive appreciation of the horizontal line.

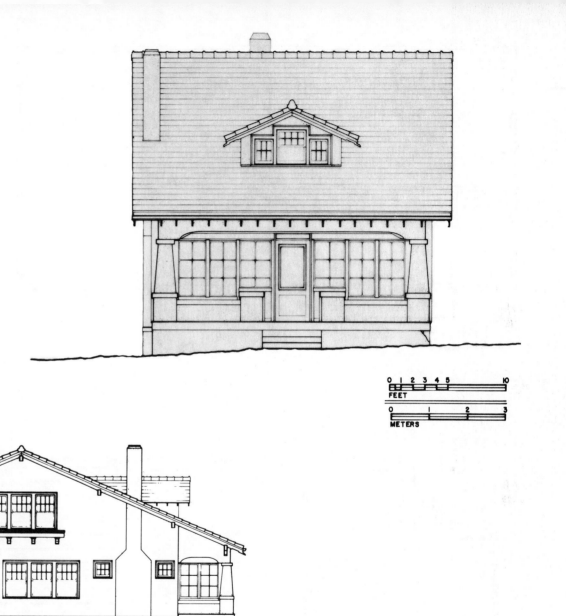

Greenhouse Manager's House, Longview Farm, Lee's Summit, Missouri, 1924, south and west elevations.

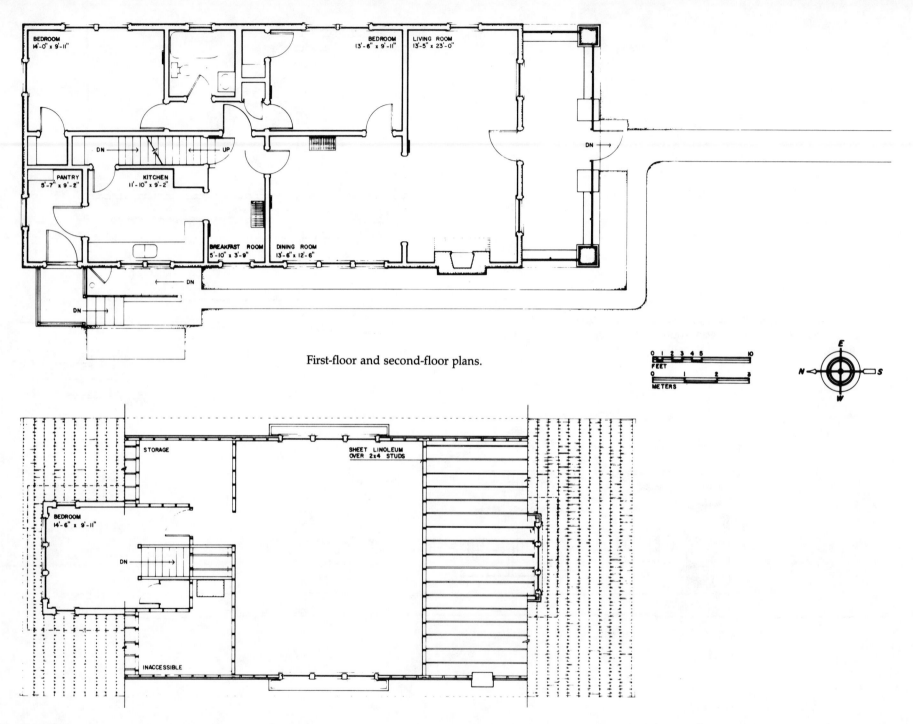

BEDROOM
14'-0" x 9'-11"

BEDROOM
13'-6" x 9'-11"

LIVING ROOM
13'-5" x 23'-0"

DN

UP

DN

PANTRY
5'-7" x 9'-2"

KITCHEN
11'-10" x 9'-2"

BREAKFAST ROOM
5'-10" x 3'-9"

DINING ROOM
13'-6" x 12'-6"

DN

DN

First-floor and second-floor plans.

0 1 2 3 4 5 10
FEET

0 1 2 3
METERS

STORAGE

SHEET LINOLEUM
OVER 2x4 STUDS

BEDROOM
14'-6" x 9'-11"

DN

INACCESSIBLE

Hanchett Residence Park, San Jose, California, 1909-12, southeast street elevation.

1257   1249   1241   1233   1225

FEET   0 5 10 15 20 25 FT
METERS   0 1 2 3 4 5 M

The Theodore Irwin House, Pasadena, California, 1906,
Charles and Henry Greene, architects, west elevation.

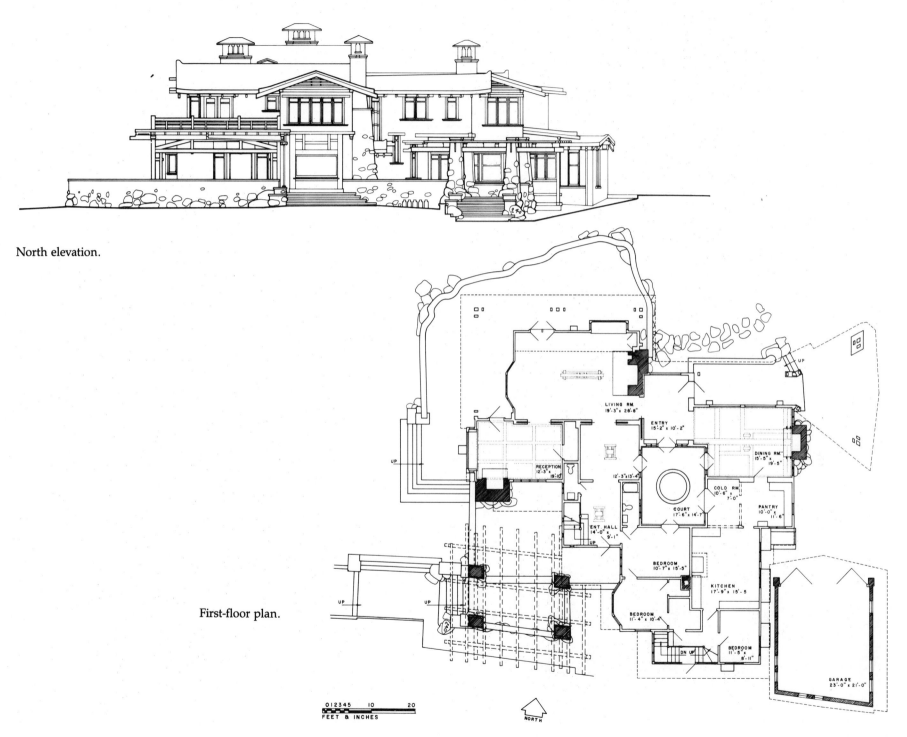

North elevation.

First-floor plan.

LIVING RM.
19'-3" x 26'-8"

ENTRY
15'-2" x 10'-2"

RECEPTION
12'-3" x
19'-10"

DINING RM.
15'-5" x
19'-5"

12'-3" x 13'-4"

COLD RM.
10'-6" x
7'-0"

COURT
17'-6" x 14'-7"

PANTRY
10'-0" x
11'-6"

ENT. HALL
14'-0" x
9'-1"

BEDROOM
10'-7" x 15'-5"

KITCHEN
17'-9" x 15'-5

BEDROOM
11'-4" x 10'-4"

BEDROOM
11'-5" x
8'-11"

DN UP

GARAGE
23'-0" x 21'-0"

0 1 2 3 4 5   10   20
FEET & INCHES

NORTH

Second-floor plan.

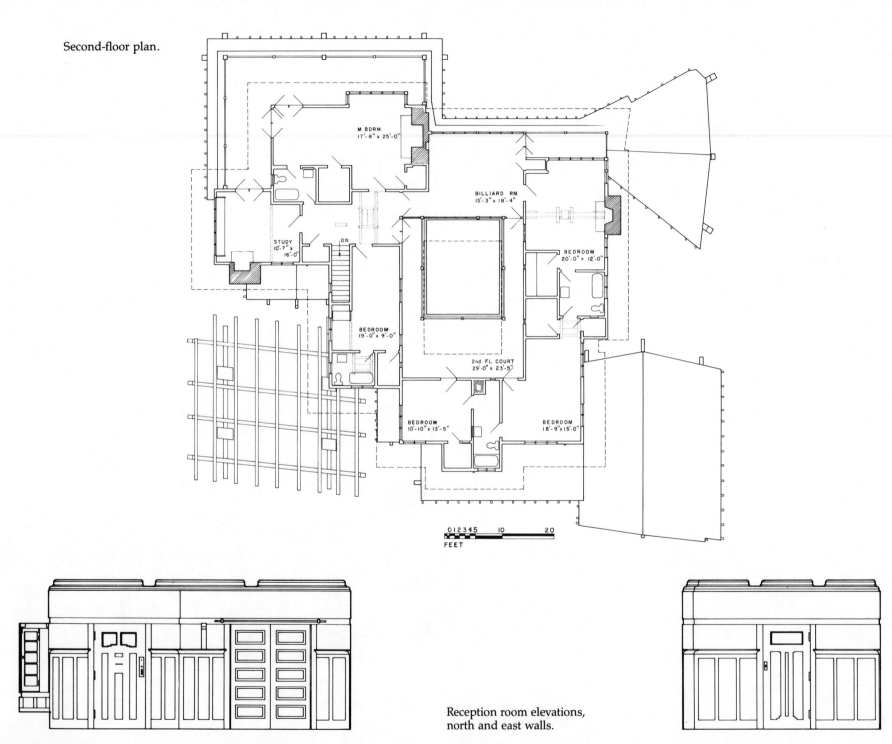

M BDRM.
17'-6" x 25'-0"

BILLIARD RM.
15'-3" x 18'-4"

STUDY
10'-7" x
16'-0"

DN

BEDROOM
20'-0" x 12'-0"

BEDROOM
19'-0" x 9'-0"

2nd. FL. COURT
29'-0" x 23'-5"

BEDROOM
10'-10" x 13'-5"

BEDROOM
18'-9" x 15'-0"

0 1 2 3 4 5   10   20
FEET

Reception room elevations,
north and east walls.

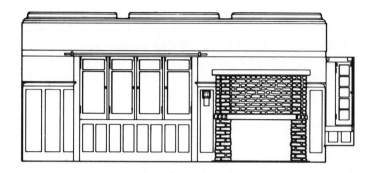

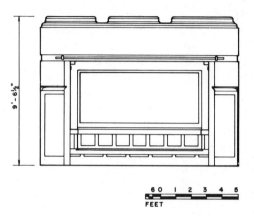

Reception room elevations,
south and west walls.

9'-6½"

60 1 2 3 4 5
FEET

Sectional view.

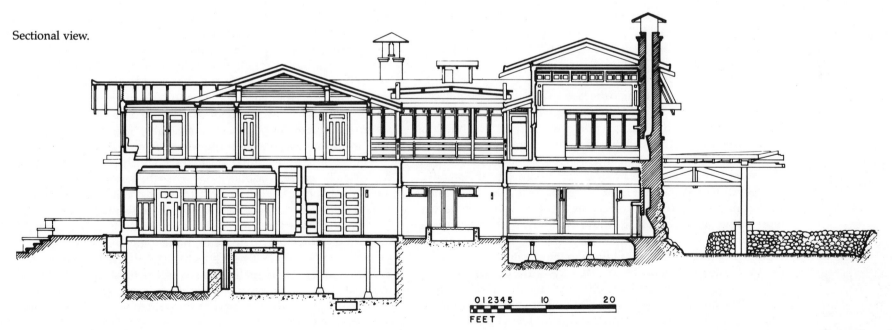

012345   10   20
FEET

Residents of America's East Coast frequently need reminding that a second and parallel tradition to English Colonial exists in the Spanish Colonial and Mission styles. This is especially ironic considering the fact that many thousands of so-called "Spanish Colonial" homes were built in the residential areas of the East during the early twentieth century. In fact, imitating the Hispanic spirit in building was as much a national craze of the 1920s as the game of mah-jongg. Suitable models—mission churches, ranch houses, forts in a Mexican baroque tradition—existed long before the West and Southwest were anglicized. These adobe brick structures are rarely found except in the last settled areas of New Mexico, Arizona, and southern California, but the romantic spirit which suffuses such a best-selling novel as Willa Cather's *Death Comes for the Archbishop* (1927), set amidst the old-world charm of Santa Fe, transcends time and place. Americans have excelled at movie sets and in adapting the past to their present needs for charm and comfort.

Little attention was paid during the revival of Spanish Colonial to the subtleties of the tradition. As in any vernacular rendering, a nonconformist has been at work. The Georgian Style easily slips into the early English Colonial; the Mansard to the Queen Anne; and the Mission to the Spanish Colonial Revival. Historians tell us that the Mission Style thrived from 1890 to 1920 and is recognized by a simplicity of form and lack of surface decoration. Yet, the so-called Spanish Colonial Revival style of 1915-1940, based on the original style of the 1600-1840 period, was often presented in a similar manner. For every example in American architectural history, there is an exception.

Interest in the Spanish Colonial past was first awakened in the West, particularly California, in the last years of the nineteenth century. It was a style well suited for important buildings such as town halls, railroad stations, and, of course, the church. The missions which stretch along the Pacific coast were and are the most obvious reminders of the now-distant and therefore romantic past. A Mission style in the decorative arts was accompanied by the architectural revival. By World War I, the initial impulse of this movement was spent, and in its place soon came a second awakening that was more pointedly directed to the home-building market throughout the country.

Some Spanish Colonial buildings in temperate areas make ample use of one prominent feature of the style—the patio. Floor plans are shaped to draw the resident into this pleasant enclosure. Homes built in the North, of course, are often without this key element. All buildings, however, do share at least a few of the following features—flat or low pitched red- or blue-tiled roofs, arched en-

tryways or arcades, and white stucco or smooth plastered walls. Wrought- or cast-iron window grilles and railings appear on some homes; exterior walls often carry baroque plaster ornamentation (see p. 115).

The O'Brien Court houses (pp. 109-112) are charming in their modesty and style. "The real Spanish or 'Southern California' style of home built in any part of the United States today," a '20s critic writes, "must have a patio if it is to be true to form. Even now we find the patio useful in many delightful ways." The positioning of the patio or courtyard at the front of the O'Brien houses is one of their inspired features. The usual position of the garden area is at the back of the house, away from the noise of the road. Here the patio provides a handsome walled courtyard through which to enter the house.

From the perspective of the 1980s, one is struck by the unusual degree of variety presented by these three adjoining buildings, all part of a real estate development. The façade of each is markedly different, but because of the common material used (stucco on wood frame) the buildings are complementary. Each has a flat roof, as befits a semi-arid climate, and red tile trim is used to accent various architectural elements. How these buildings differ in floor plan is not known, but they may follow the general lines seen in the 1928 "Spanish Bungalow" (pp. 113-114). The two sections of the L-shaped bungalow, however, are more clearly separated than the components of the development houses.

This bungalow is typical of a common type of Spanish Colonial Revival house built throughout the United States in the early 1900s. There is a gable rather than a flat roof, and terraces (at front and rear) have taken the place of the patio. The stuccoed walls, deep window reveals, massive recessed door, and tile roofing, however, stamp the style of this house as unmistakably Spanish. The interior appointments carry through the romantic revival style.

A house such as the bungalow in the Spanish Colonial tradition has virtually ceased to be built today while the various step-children and orphans of the English Colonial tradition continue to proliferate. This is a distinct loss because the style is well-suited to vast areas of the North American continent and lends itself most readily to modern interpretation. The clean, handsome designs of California architects of the 1920s such as Irving Gill, Wallace Neff, and Bernard Maybeck anticipated the spare structuralism of the International Style but, in the opinion of many, successfully mixed the comfort of a graceful tradition with the demands of modern life for convenience in a way that has never been equalled.

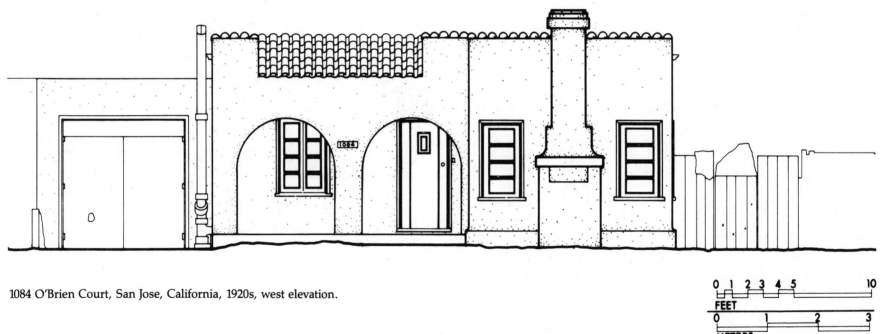

1084 O'Brien Court, San Jose, California, 1920s, west elevation.

0 1 2 3 4 5   10
FEET
0   1   2   3
METERS

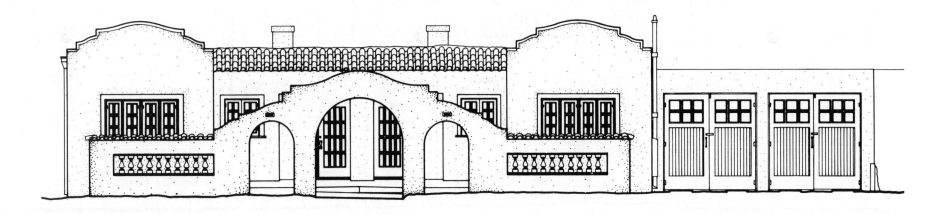

1076-1078 O'Brien Court, San Jose, California, 1920s, west elevation.

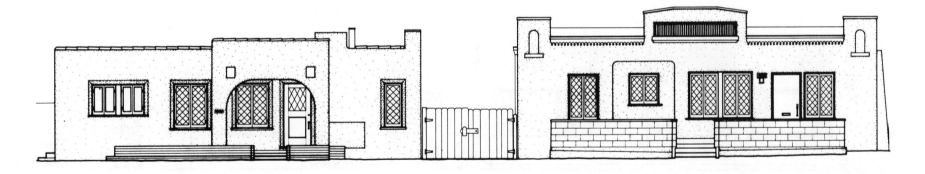

1086-1088 O'Brien Court, San Jose, California, 1920s, west elevation.

1090-1092 O'Brien Court, San Jose, California, 1920s, west elevation.

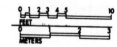

"Spanish Bungalow" design, 1928, perspective.

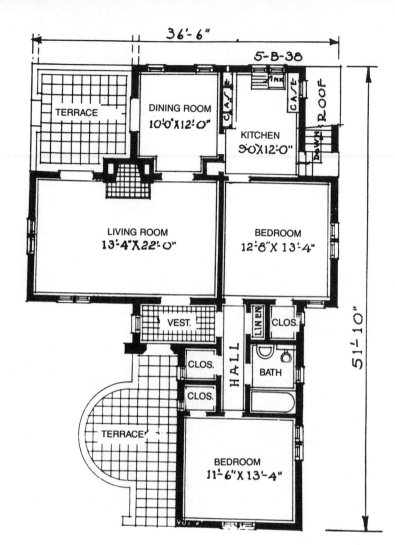

Floor plan and living room perspective.

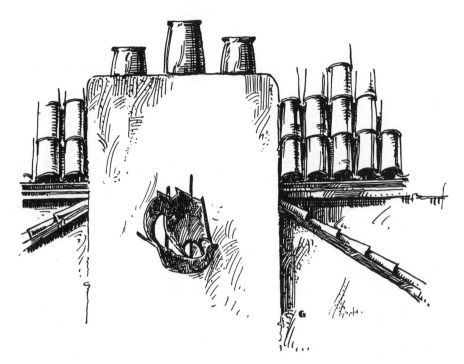

Typical exterior details of Spanish Colonial Revival homes.

What the early settlers achieved in architectural simplicity, their descendants "improved" upon. As with many other revivals, that of the Colonial was an attempt to recapture a style of the past which had nostalgic appeal and symbolic importance. Colonial Revival is Georgian Colonial writ large in columned porticoes, Palladian and bow-front windows, massive brick chimneys, and elaborate exterior and interior millwork. Following the Centennial, interest in replicating the Colonial heritage slowly grew in strength. During the 1880s and '90s some of the most fashionable architects in New York and Boston carefully reproduced Georgian features in homes, club houses, and churches. By the 1920s, when Williamsburg was first hatched, the Colonial Revival became as middle class as Dick and Jane's red brick house. In the post-World War II period, it invaded the countryside in Howard Johnson subdivision form, and there it has stayed—America's true architectural sweetheart.

Now over 100 years old, Colonial Revival has in itself become antique. It is hard, however, to envision historic status being granted at some future time to a majority of the 1980s home being built in the Neo-Colonial tradition. The Colonial Revival ran out of steam by the 1920s in terms of stylistic integrity and handling of materials. Some architectural historians would probably claim that only the very first buildings in this style by Arthur Little, McKim, Mead and White, and Charles A. Platt qualify for serious study. Our concern in *Classic Old House Plans,* however, is not with the stylistically pure but with the vernacular. Yet a number of experts look back with some admiration on the later practitioners of the style. As Marcus Whiffen notes in *American Architecture Since 1780,* "the Neo-Adamesque façades that went up in such numbers along the streets of New York and other cities in the 1920s constitute the last consistent street architecture that America has had."

Whiffen points out that architects working in this style depended on two traditions for their inspiration—the Georgian Colonial and the Federal. The Neo-Federal or Neo-Adamesque proportions and detailing, as pointed out elsewhere in this book, relate strongly to the Neo-Colonial. As the Federal was an appropriate style for urban town houses in the early nineteenth century, so, too, was it adopted and adapted in Eastern cities during the early years of the twentieth century. In suburban and rural areas, Georgian Colonial and even earlier and more rustic versions of the domestic vernacular were the order of the day. As is evident in the Wharton-Scott house plan (pp. 117-120) the dimensions of the average house are considerably greater than those found in either most middle eighteenth-century or mid-twentieth-century Colonials.

The magnificent Wharton-Scott House would have suited the taste of a millionaire in Massachusetts as well as in Texas. From the base of the double-story portico to the tip of the main gambrel-roofed section, little expense could have been spared. Everything is larger than life. The center entry hall is at least twice as wide as the average eighteenth-century hallway. It leads to a grand staircase which divides into two sections at a mid-floor landing. Opening off the entry foyer and hall are a drawing room, library, music room, and dining room. Behind these rooms are the kitchen and a breakfast room. The second floor is similarly lavish in proportions, with four bedrooms, two baths, two dressing rooms, and a garden room.

The basic floor plan is cruciform rather than rectangular, thus allowing for a greater variety in the shape and character of the rooms than the traditional Colonial arrangement. Curved and pilastered walls are graceful features of the dining room and music room as well as the bedrooms immediately above them. Five towering chimneys provide flues for kitchen, drawing room, library, music room, dining room, and bedroom fireplaces. The mansion is bathed in natural light from larger than usual windows, most of them double-sash rather than the many-paned variety found in true Colonial-period dwellings.

The New Jersey suburban homes shown on pages 121 and 122 are modest in comparison to the Wharton-Scott House. Each building incorporates stylish details of the Georgian Colonial/Federal periods, including applied decoration, balustrades, and neoclassical columns. Both are clapboard frame houses which were undoubtedly painted white.

The 1922 Georgian Colonial residence (pp. 123-124) more faithfully follows historical tradition. It is a purely symmetrical five-bay building with a center pedimented entryway on the first floor and a Palladian window above. The center hall provides access to all the rooms in the main rectangular block and leads to the service ell at the rear. There are several obvious features of the residence which testify to its twentieth-century origins: the narrow clapboarding, double-sash windows, louvered shutters, and side piazza. The floor plan also says a great deal about modern times as it includes three baths. Even if we did not know the date of the house, however, we would be aware that its building had to predate World War II, for provision is made for three servants' rooms on the second floor.

Details in other Georgian Colonial Revival homes included exterior clapboarding, shingling, stuccoing, and fieldstone facing. Clapboards ranged in width from about nine to three-and-a-half inches. Roofs were often of the hip variety, and sometimes included a balustraded deck. A Palladian window was frequently centered at the second-story level in a pediment which broke the roof line. Interior detailing might include wainscoting, the use of chair rails, and elaborate fireplace wall and doorway moldings. Some houses in suburban areas of New England and of the Middle Atlantic states were so successful in their reproduction of the Colonial that only a dating of structural materials will establish a building's true age.

The historical importance of the Georgian Colonial Revival house should not be exaggerated. In the hands of a master architect, however, a dwelling of considerable grace and strength emerged with a distinct and valid style. Denver, Colorado, has established the first historic landmark district of such homes; others in time— if saved—will take their place on the registries of architecturally significant buildings.

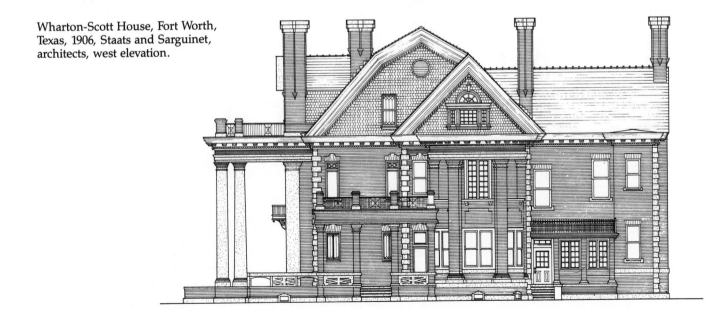

Wharton-Scott House, Fort Worth, Texas, 1906, Staats and Sarguinet, architects, west elevation.

FEET 0 [   ] 10
METERS 0 [   ] 5

Sectional view (west).

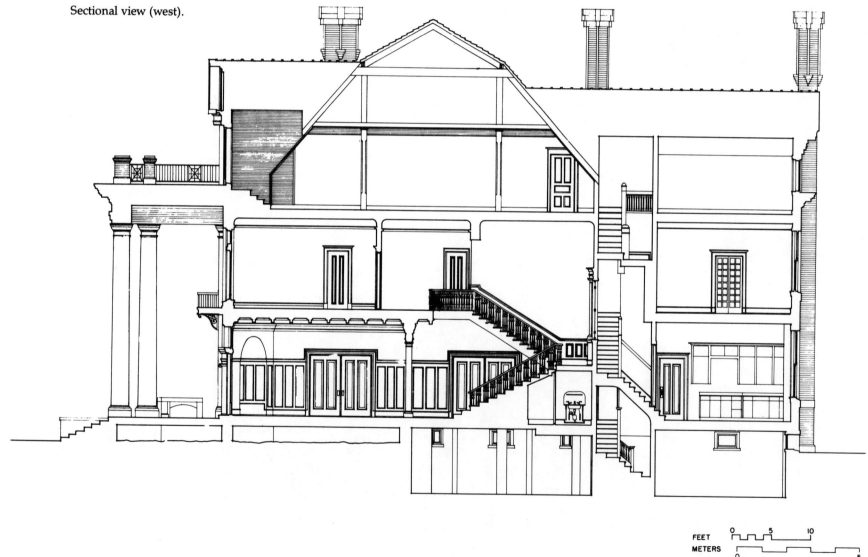

FEET   0   5   10

METERS 0   5

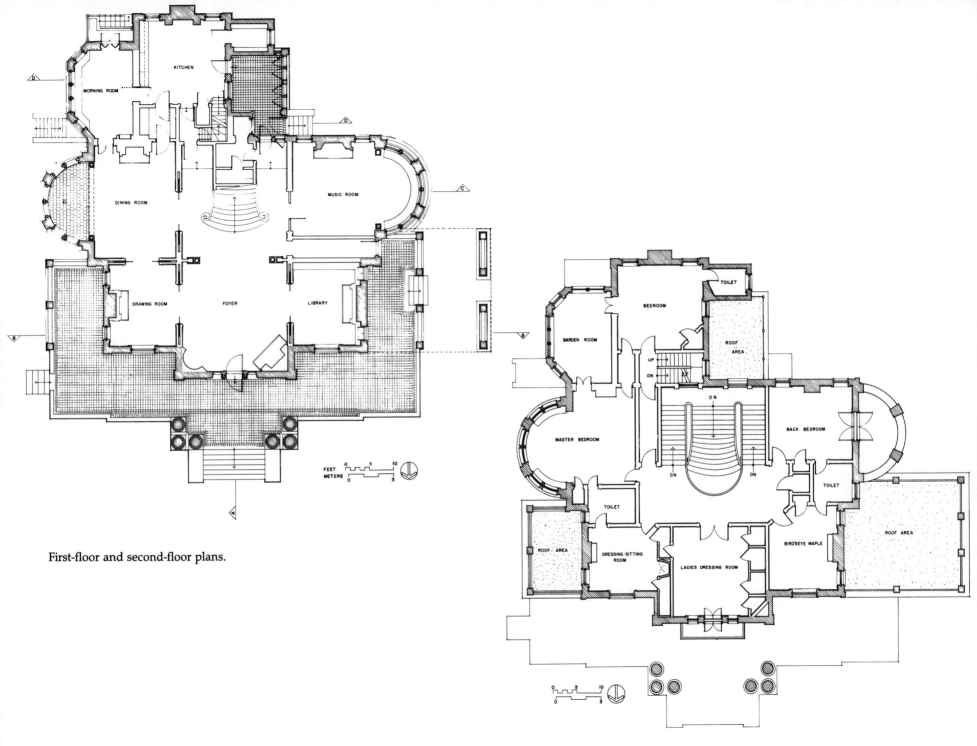

KITCHEN

MORNING ROOM

DINING ROOM

MUSIC ROOM

DRAWING ROOM

FOYER

LIBRARY

FEET
METERS
0 5 10
0 3

First-floor and second-floor plans.

BEDROOM

TOILET

GARDEN ROOM

ROOF AREA

UP
DN

DN

MASTER BEDROOM

BACK BEDROOM

DN

DN

TOILET

TOILET

ROOF AREA

DRESSING·SITTING ROOM

LADIES DRESSING ROOM

BIRD'S·EYE MAPLE

ROOF AREA

0 5 10
0 3

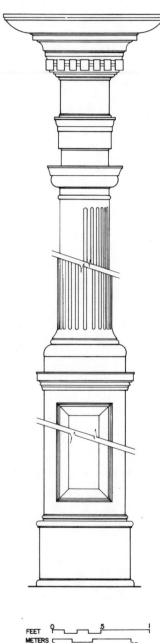

Stair landing details.

FEET 0 5
METERS 0 .25

Residence, Glen Ridge, New Jersey, 1901,
William A. Lambert, architect, perspective.

L. K. Hazard House, Elizabeth, New Jersy,
1892, A. L. C. March, architect, perspective.

"Georgian Colonial" residence, 1922, perspective.

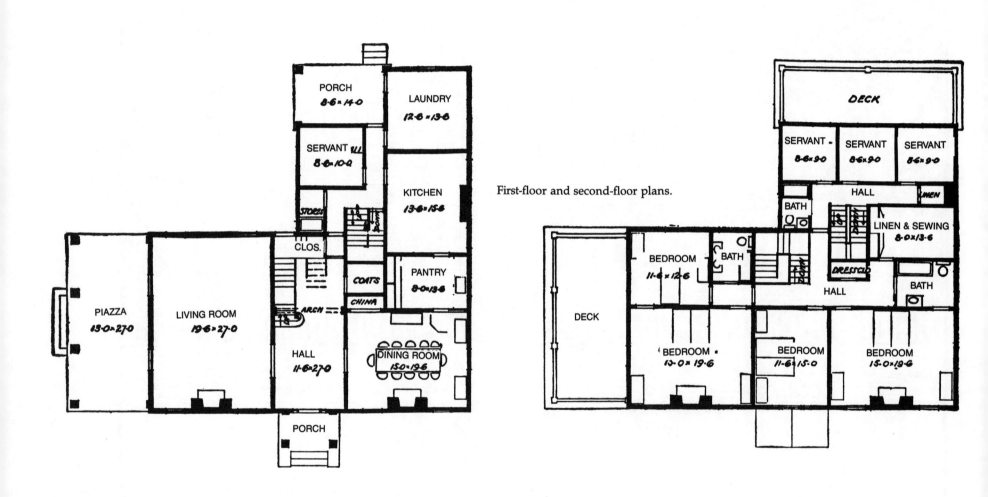

First-floor and second-floor plans.

PORCH
8-6 x 14-0

LAUNDRY
12-6 x 13-6

SERVANT
8-6 x 10-0

KITCHEN
13-6 x 15-6

STORE

CLOS.

PANTRY
8-0 x 13-6

PIAZZA
13-0 x 27-0

LIVING ROOM
19-6 x 27-0

COATS

CHINA

ARCH

HALL
11-6 x 27-0

DINING ROOM
15-0 x 19-6

PORCH

DECK

SERVANT
8-6 x 9-0

SERVANT
8-6 x 9-0

SERVANT
8-6 x 9-0

HALL

LINEN

BATH

LINEN & SEWING
8-0 x 13-6

BEDROOM
11-6 x 12-6

BATH

DRESS CLO.

HALL

BATH

DECK

BEDROOM
13-0 x 19-6

BEDROOM
11-6 x 15-0

BEDROOM
15-0 x 19-6

Many of the homes illustrated in these pages have been studied by members of the Historic American Buildings Survey of the National Park Service, U.S. Department of the Interior, over the past fifty years. The drawings and photographs executed by members of these research teams are maintained by the Library of Congress, Washington, D.C. These materials are available to the general public and reproduction is copyright free. For information regarding any of the following drawings, inquiries should be made in writing to the Division of Prints and Photographs, Library of Congress Washington, D.C. 20450. Given with the name of the property is the HABS survey number; this is followed by the drawing number.

Colonial: Felix and Odille Pratte Vallé House (31-11) north elevation, 3-7, sectional view, 7-7, first-floor plan, 1-7, second-floor plan, 2-7; Justin Williams House (MA 703) south elevation, 1-4, first-floor plan, 2-4; Chase-Lloyd House (MD 243) southeast elevation, 5-7, elevation, 7-7, first-floor plan, 3-7; Blandfield (VA 1198) main block, 11-21, first-floor plan, 3-21, sectional view, 17-21, second-floor plan, 8-21, door detail, 21-21, mantel detail, 21-21.

Federal: Isaiah Davenport House (14-8) south and east elevations, 3-5, elevation, doorway, detail, elevation, arch, 5-5; William Scarbrough House (GA 2127) east elevation, 7-22, first-floor plan, 4-22, second-floor plan, 5-22.

Greek Revival: Campbell-Whittlesey House (5-R-6) north elevation, 2-12, first and second floor plans, 1-12; Skinner-Trowbridge House (CONN 272) east elevation, 7-7, first-floor plan, 2-7; René Beauregard House (18-7) southwest elevation, 4-9; James F. D. Lanier Home (IND 23) south elevation, portico, column, and steps details, 5-15, west elevation, 8-15, transverse section, 9-15, stair elevation, 14-15, first-floor plan, 2-15; Andrews-Taylor House (TEX 147) west elevation, 4-11, first-floor plan, 2-11, second-floor plan, 3-11.

Gothic Revival: A. B. Austin House (ILL 280) east entrance, 3-3, first-floor and second-floor plans, 2-3, east elevation, 1-3.

Italianate: Morse-Libby House (ME 53) front elevation, 2-2, first-floor and second-floor plans, 1-2, third-floor plan, 2-2; Willis Bristol House (CONN 274) north elevation, 4-6, first-floor plan, 2-6; Residence (Austin) (TEX 3266) south elevation (no number available), window and doorway details, 5-6, site and floor plans, 2-6, sectional view (no number available).

Second Empire/Mansard: Captain's Cottage No. 2 (NY 6244) east elevation, 4-6, cross section, 6-6, basement floor plan, 1-6, first-floor plan, 2-6, second-floor plan, 3-6; Captain Edward Penniman House (MASS 693) west elevation, 9-9, first-floor plan, 4-9, second-floor plan, 5-9, sectional view, 8-9.

Queen Anne: Alfred Uihlein House (WIS 253) sectional view, 8-10, south elevation, 7-10, first-floor plan, 2-10, fireplace elevation, 10-10, second-floor plan, 3-10, third-floor plan, 4-10, door elevation, plan, profiles, 10-11; John B. Lindale House (DE 172) south elevation, 3-4, first-floor and second-floor plans, 2-4.

Shingle: Isaac Bell House (RI 308) east elevation, 4-8, first-floor and second-floor plans, 2-8, fireplace elevation, 3-8.

Romanesque: Ira A. Heath House (ILL 1066) east elevation, 3-3, first-floor and second-floor plans, 2-3; Elizabeth Plankinton House (WI 280) south elevation, 5-12, first-floor plan, 2-12, second-floor plan, 3-12, third-floor plan, 4-12, sectional view, 8-12.

English Tudor: Alan M. Scaife Residence (PA 620) west elevation, 8-12, first-floor plan, 4-12, second-floor plan, 5-12.

Bungalow: Greenhouse Manager's House (MO 1222-27) south and west elevations, 1-2, first-floor and second-floor plans, 2-2; Hanchett Residence Park (CA 2010) 4-4; Theodore Irwin House (CAL 1931) west elevation, 6-14, north elevation, 6-14, first-floor plan, 4-14, second-floor plan, 5-14, reception room elevations, 1-14, sectional view, 8-14.

Spanish Colonial Revival: 1076-92 O'Brien Court (CA 2106) 1084 west elevation, 2-3, 1076-78 west elevation, 2-3, 1086-88, west elevation, 3-3, 1090-92, west elevation, 3-3.

Georgian Colonial Revival: Wharton-Scott House (TX 3289) west elevation, no number available, sectional view, no number available, first-floor plan, no number available, second-floor plan, no number available, stair landing details, no number available.